THE EARLY FRENCH POETS

THE EARLY FRENCH POETS

By HENRY FRANCIS CARY

Translator of Dante, with an Introduction by
T. Earle Welby . . . . .

KENNIKAT PRESS
Port Washington, N. Y./London

THE EARLY FRENCH POETS

First published in 1923
Reissued in 1970 by Kennikat Press
Library of Congress Catalog Card No: 72-103219
SBN 8046-0856-3

Manufactured by Taylor Publishing Company   Dallas, Texas

Contents

Introduction

—

THE Rev. Henry Francis Cary, who was born in 1772 and died in 1844, and who published renderings of Dante, 1805-1814, Pindar, 1824, and the " Birds " of Aristophanes, 1824, is universally honoured as a translator, but on account of one only of his several admirable translations. His Dante has been constantly reprinted; his not less scholarly and effective translations from " The Early French Poets," collected two years after his death, have been allowed to fall into complete neglect.

They constitute a book very well worth rescuing. As a critical and biographical introduction to the whole subject it remains, for all the sketchiness of certain sections, the most agreeable and useful that we have. No doubt almost everyone to-day is cleverer about portions of this subject than anyone could be in Cary's day. The essays here reprinted, though not collected till 1846, were written to journalistic occasions between 1821 and 1825 : Cary was a pioneer, with very little French and no English guidance. He could not return to the original French of Villon with his faculty of appreciation quickened by perusal of marvellous translations by Rossetti and Swinburne. He did not, like Andrew Lang, find English verse prepared, by Rossetti and Swinburne, and in another way by FitzGerald, for the task of rendering exotic beauty into our language. He worked before both those French scholars who have lessened our ignorance of Villon's career, of Ronsard's aims, and those English writers who, like the late George Wyndham and Mr. Hilaire Belloc, have dealt summarily with old French poetry for the ordinary reader in this country.   At some points Cary's biographical or bibliographical knowledge is inadequate ; but it is usually ample for his purpose.   Of some writers he fails to give us the *vraie verité* ; but he is nowhere insensitive or extravagant, he is often acute, and in prose as good as his verse he has the method most to be desired in an introductory work.   He says of Pierre Gringore : " The style is of the homeliest throughout ; but there is the good meaning of the writer, worthy the age of Louis the Just, and here and there an arch phrase, or a quaint old word, cunningly set, to repay the reader for his trouble."   In sentences like that there is a way of doing generous justice expeditiously such as this kind of book requires. With Villon he fell altogether short, seeming never to have perceived, while he noted the " happy turns of expression, smart personalities and witty innuendoes," the intensity of imagination and smiting directness of phrase which make Villon one of the supreme lyric poets of the world.   But his version of Villon's " Ballade of the Ladies of Past Time " is done with a sympathy and fidelity quite astonishing for work of the Byronic or Mooreish era in which Moore could be supposed capable of reproducing Catullus.

In that version as often elsewhere with Cary, the translator has some of the courage of his original.   Bad translators lack it, and will go about to make more

" poetical " some simplicity of their author. Rossetti was not a bad, he was an almost uniquely supple and accomplished translator, and outside his lovely poems from the Italian he never did anything better than this ballade of Villon's ; but it was not altogether unreasonably that W. E. Henley charged him with making Villon a resident of Bedford Park. There are touches too " æsthetic " in the beautiful and on the whole very faithful version. It is beautiful verse, and how ingenious in finding a rhyme for " Thais " ! But " in what hidden way is " gives to the opening a particularity more characteristic of Rossetti than of Villon, who was content with the general " *pays*." Again, there is " yesteryear," an unnatural word for Villon's quite natural " *antan*," and not to be excused as conveying Villon's exact meaning, for " *antan* " is *ante annum*, not " yesteryear " but " all the years before this year." I cannot suppose that Cary, if he had attempted it, would have done the great Ballade of the regrets of " la belle qui fut heaulmière " with anything like the imaginative ardour and triumphant ease of Swinburne, but neither would he have persuaded himself that Villon wrote the equivalent of " red splendid kissing mouth."

But, to return to things actually translated by Cary, the reader may profit by comparing his versions with those of Lang, of Wyndham and of other systematic or casual translators.

When Cary's essays on the old French poets were collected by his son, that capable editor found it impossible to place them in chronological order of subjects without many alterations in the text. These he was indisposed—and we should not be entitled—to make.

He prefixed to the essays a preliminary sketch of early French poetry in which the poets dealt with in the essays, and many others, were noticed in sequence. I doubt whether such an outline of the history of French poetry is now needed, and it seems to me likely that the reader who wished to go beyond Cary's own work would demand a much ampler treatment, in the light of later research and criticism. The younger Cary's introductory matter has therefore been excluded from this reprint, which otherwise reproduces the critical and biographical matter of the volume of 1846, my editorial interference with its text being limited to the correction of two or three misprints or errors in transcription and the excision of lengthy quotations. The dates of the writers have been introduced under the titles of the essays, and for the rest all the chronology required by the reader of this delightful book would seem to be contained in the reminder that chronologically the book should begin with the subject of the second essay, Thibaut, King of Navarre, more than two hundred years before Villon, and conclude with Jean Bertaut, more than a hundred years after Villon. The end of the old French poetry came when Malherbe, born in 1555, thirty-one years after Ronsard, came to Court.

> Enfin Malherbe vint, et le premier en France,
> Fit sentir dans les vers une juste cadence,
> D'un mot mis à sa place enseigna le pouvoir,
> Et réduisit la Muse aux règles du devoir.

T. EARLE WELBY

CLEMENT MAROT

1484-1544

IN the course of this last summer, I happened to reside
for some weeks in a place where I had free access
to a large collection of books,* which formerly
belonged to the kings of France, but, like other royal
property, having been confiscated at the Revolution, still
continues unreclaimed, and is now open to the use of the
public. Of this occasion I gladly availed myself to
extend my acquaintance with some of their earlier
writers, whose works are not commonly to be met
with in our own country ; and, amongst these, fixed my
attention principally on such of their poets as were of
most note at the restoration or, more properly speaking,
the general diffusion of polite learning in Europe.
What the result of this enquiry has been I invite my
readers to judge.

The French of the present day, I know, set but little
store on these revivers of the poetical art. Their extreme
solicitude for what they call the purity of their language
makes them easily offended by phrases the irregularities
of which we should be ready to pardon in consideration

* At Versailles, where the Author spent the summer of 1821.—
ED.

of higher excellence or even to welcome as so many means of aiding us in that escape from the tameness of common everyday life which it is one great end of poetry to effect. I do not know of any other people who have set up an exclusive standard of this sort. What would the Greeks of the age of Pericles have said to a literary censor that should have endeavoured to persuade them to throw aside the works of Homer and Hesiod because he could have pointed out to them in every page modes of expression that would not have passed muster in a coterie at Aspasia's? What reply should we make to a critic that would fain put us out of conceit with some of the finest things in Spenser and Shakespeare because they were cast in a mould utterly differing from that impressed on the language of our politer circles, though similar enough to the stamp of our country-folks' talk? Let anyone take up Voltaire's commentary on the tragedies of Corneille and he will see to what a pitch this fastidiousness has been carried in the instance of a writer comparatively modern. I am not much afraid lest the generality of my readers should be subject to any such disgust. Our ignorance is a happy security from this danger, though I trust it will not prevent us from being alive to the many beauties that will meet us in the search we are about to engage in.

We will begin with Marot : not because his works are of very rare occurrence (for there have been many editions of them), but because, though frequently spoken of, and even recommended as a model of elegant " badinage " by Boileau, he is but little known amongst us ; which indeed is not much to be wondered at when his own countrymen seem to have almost lost sight of him. " Marot is much talked of, but seldom read," says one of their critics.* " We do not read with pleasure that which has need of a dictionary to explain it. Almost all his expressions are antiquated." " Villon and Marot, and some others, are satirical poets ; and their epigrams may be said to be the only titles they have to celebrity in the present day," says another.† All this may show the little taste the French now have for their elder poets. How otherwise could they have overlooked those exquisite sketches, the Temple of Cupid, and the Eclogue of Pan and Robin, by Marot : the latter of which is worthy the author of the Faerie Queene,‡ as the former is of Chaucer ?

We might almost suppose ourselves to be reading an imitation of the poem to the Canterbury Tales in the following verses with which the Temple of Cupid opens :

> Sur le printemps que la belle Flora
> Les champs couverts de diverse fleur a,
> E son amy Zephyrus les esvente,
> Quand doucement en l'air souspire e vente.

The whole poem is indeed so fanciful, and so replete with a peculiar kind of sprightly humour, that I am

* M. Dussault, in a review of a selection of Marot's Works, inserted in his Annales Littéraires, t.i., p. 198.

† M. Avenel, one of the writers in the Lycée Francais, t.ii., p. 106, an entertaining miscellany that lasted but a short time after the decease of Charles Loyson, a young poet of considerable promise, who was a chief contributor to it. He died in the course of last year.

‡ Indeed he has closely copied it in the Shepheard's Kalendar, Ecl. 12.

not without hopes of amusing my readers by an abstract of it.

In this merry spring-tide, the god commands that his eyes may be unbandaged, and looking round his celestial throne sees all nations bending under his sway, like a scion under the wind ; and the other deities themselves submitting to his power. But, observing that Marot continued still refractory, he resolves to tame the rebel ; and, taking an arrow out of his quiver, executes his purpose so effectually as to render the unhappy poet an object of commiseration to all who have a heart capable of pity. In order to assuage his sufferings, Marot resolves on a far-off journey in search of the goddess Ferme-amour, a pure and chaste dame, whom Jupiter had sent upon earth, committing the government of loyal spirits to her care. A long time did the poet compass land and sea, like a knight-errant, on this quest. Of all to whom he came he enquired whether she dwelt in their land ; but of none did he gain any tidings of her. At length he determines to go to the Temple Cupidique, in the hopes of finding her there ; and, setting out early in the morning, has no difficulty in discovering his way ; for many a passing pilgrim had sprinkled it with roses and branches of rosemary ; and, as he advanced, he fell in with other pilgrims who journeyed on, sighing and relating their sad haps. Joining their company, he arrives with them at the royal temple ; where, in the enclosure that surrounded it, the sweet breath of the west-wind, and Tytyrus, and the god Pan with his flocks and herds, and the sound of pipes and flageolets, and of birds answering to them, soon refreshed his wearied spirits.

Tous arbres sont en ce lieu verdoyans ;
Petits ruisseaux y furent ondoyans,
Toujours faisans, au tour des prez herbus
Un doux murmure : et quand le cler Phebus
Avoit droit là ses beaux rayons espars,
Telle splendeur rendoit de toutes pars
Ce lieu divin, qu'aux humains bien sembloit
Que terre au ciel de beauté ressembloit.

His heart assured him that this was the residence of
Ferme-amour ; and Hope led him onward to the delightful
place. It seemed as if Jove had come from heaven on
purpose to frame it ; and there was wanting nothing but
Adam and Eve to make one believe that it was the
terrestrial paradise itself.

Over the portal he observed a scutcheon with the arms
of Love engraved on it ; and higher up the figure of Cupid
himself, with his naked bow outstretched and ready to
discharge an arrow at the first comer. He now enters ;
and is welcomed by Bel-accueil, who takes him by his
right hand, and leads him through a narrow path
into the beautiful enclosure of which he was the first
porter.

The door was built up of all flowers red
And buds, that from their buttons issued,
Denoting well that joys without compare
For ever in that place y-blooming were.

This was the barrier kept by Bel-accueil in his green
robe ; who day and night opens to true lovers and
gracious ; and willingly enlists them under his banners ;

whilst he excludes (as reason is) all those who are such as the perfidious and disloyal Jason.

We now come to the great altar, which is a rock of that virtue that every lover who would flee from it is drawn nearer, like steel to the magnet.   The canopy is a cedar, which stretches so wide as to cover the altar, on which body, and heart, and goods, must be given up as an offering to Venus.

> On Cupid's brow for crown was set
> Of roses a fair chapelet,
> The which within her garden green
> Were gather'd by Love's gracious queen,
> And by her to her infant dear
> Sent in the spring-time of the year.
> These he with right good-will did don ;
> And to his mother thereupon
> A chariot gave, in trumph led
> By turtles twelve all harnessed.
> Before the altar saw I, blooming fair,
> Two cypresses, embalm'd with odours rare.
> And these, quoth they, are pillars that do bide
> To stay this altar famed far and wide.
> And then a thousand birds upon the wing
> Amid those curtains green came fluttering,
> Ready to sing their little songs divine.
> And so I ask'd, why came they to that shrine ?
> And these, they said, are matins, friend ; which they
> In honour of Love's queen are come to say.

Before the image of Cupid burned the brand of Distress, " le brandon de Destresse," with which Dido,

Biblis, and Helen of Greece, were inflamed. Now, however, it served as a lamp to the temple.

The saints of either sex, who are invoked here, are Beau-parler, Bien-celer, Bon-rapport, Grace, Marcy, Bien-servir, Bien-aymer, and others, without whose aid no pilgrim can succeed in overtaking the prey which he pursues in the Forest of Loves.

> Torches quench'd or flaming high,
> That all loving pilgrims bear
> Before the saints that list their prayer,
> Are posies made of rosemary,
>   Many a linnet and canary,
> And many a gay nightingale,
> Amid the green-wood's leafy shroud,
> Instead of desks on branches smale,*
> For verse, response, and 'pistle loud,
> Sit shrilling of their merry song.
>   The windows were of crystal clear,
> On which old gestes depeinten are,
> Of such as with true hearts did hold
> The laws by Love ordain'd of old.

In secret tabernacles and little shrines are deposited necklaces, rings, crowns (coins), ducats, and chains of gold ; by which greater miracles are wrought in love than even by the mighty saint Beau-parler (Fine-talk) himself.

The vaults and arches are marvellously interlaced with trellis-work of vines, from which the young buds and grapes are seen depending.

* This reminds one of a line in Shakespeare's sonnets :
" Bare ruin'd choirs where late the sweet birds sang."

The bells are tabours, dulcimers, harps, lutes, hoboes, flageolets, trumpets, and clarions; from which, whensoever they are sounded, there issues a chime so melodious that there is no soldier, however fond of war, who would not quit lance and sabre to become a monk in this temple.

On the sick and infirm, who are recommended for charity, the ladies bestow smiles, and kind looks, and kisses, for alms. The preachers are elderly matrons, who exhort their younger sisters not to lose the flower of their age; and many are the converts that are won over by this doctrine. The cemetery is a green wood; the walls, hedges and brakes; the crosses are fruit trees; and the De Profundis, merry songs. Ovid, Master Alain Chartier, Petrarch, and the Romant of the Rose, serve for Mass-book, Breviary, and Psalter; and the lessons chaunted are rondeaux, ballads, and virelays. Other manner of chaunts there are, that consist only of cries, wailings, and complaints. The little chapels or oratories are leafy chambers and branching cabinets; labyrinths in wood and gardens, where one loses oneself while the green lasts; the wickets are low bushes, and the pavement all of green sward.

The eau-benite (or holy water) stood in a lake, called the lake of tears, made from the weeping of lovers. Nothing can grow near it; but everything there is withered throughout the year. The water-sprinkle was a faded rose. As for the incense that was burned within the temple, it was composed of daisies, pinks, amaranths, roses, rosemary, red buttons, lavender, and every flower that casts a comfortable smell; but the marigold too (the flower of care, " de le soucie ") was amongst them :

> Voila qui mi trouble le sens.

Genius, the arch-priest, stands ready to administer the vows to all who are desirous of professing. The altars, whereon they are sworn, are couches covered with sumptuous ornaments ; no candles are used day or night ; and the terms of their profession are so clear that novices know more than the most learned clerks.

The masses for requiem are serenadings ; and the solemn words repeated for the deceased, as paternosters and avemaryes, are the gossiping and prattle of women. The sacred processions are the morris-dancing, and mumming, and antic feats of amorous champions ; their consolings are to talk pair by pair, or to read the Ars Amandi for gospels ; and their holy relics are the lips of their ladies. On all sides, says Marot, I look round me and contemplate ; and in my life I think I never saw a temple so well filled at all points, excepting one— and that was, that there was no pix (paix) on the altar. Joy there is, and mourning full of wrath ; for one rest, ten travails ; and, in brief, it would be hard to say whether it were more like Hell or Paradise : I know not what to compare it to better than a rose encompassed with thorns ; short pleasures and long complainings.

After some other adventures in the temple, he at last finds Ferme-amour in the choir between a great prince and an excellent lady, who were invested with the royal fleur-de-lys and ducal ermines. Bel-accueil opens for him the entrance into the choir, and he gladly enlists himself under the standard of Ferme-amour ; but the play on the words, chœur and cœur, on which the conclusion turns, cannot be preserved in English.

It may be seen from this view of one of his poems how strong a resemblance Marot bears to Chaucer. He has the same liveliness of fancy ; the same rapidity and distinctness of pencil ; the same archness ; the same disposition to satire : but he has all these generally in a less degree. His language does not approach much nearer to the modern than old Geoffrey's, though his age is so much less remote from ours. Marot was contemporary with our writers in the time of Henry VIII ; and had they left anything equal to this piece, or to the Epistle of Maguelonne à son Amy Pierre de Provence, or to the Hero and Leander of this writer, many a lover of antique simplicity would have risen up amongst us to show how superior such compositions were to the nugæ canoræ of later times.

A passage in the last-mentioned of these poems, descriptive of the reception Hero gives her lover, after his first swimming across the Hellespont, appears to me to be a model of ease and sweetness.

> Elle embrassa d'amour et d'aise pleine
> Son cher espoux quasi tout hors d'aleine,
> Ayant encor ses blancs cheveux mouillez
> Tous degouttans, et d'escume souillez
> Lors le mena dedans son cabinet ;
> Et quand son corps eut essuyé bien net,
> D'huile rosat bien odorant l'oignit,
> Et de la mer le senteur estainguit.*

* It will be found on a comparison with the Greek poem of Musæus that Marot has followed it very closely. I have not Marlow and Chapman's poem, lately re-edited with a pleasant preface, nor Mr. Elton's translation, to compare with this.

Du Bellay, a poet who lived in Marot's time, considered his Eclogue on the Birth of the Dauphin as one of his best productions. It is little more than a translation of the Pollio of Virgil.

His tale of the Lion and Rat opened the way for La Fontaine's excellence in that species of writing.

The epigrams, for which he is so much applauded, are often gross and licentious. I have selected one that is not open to this objection.

> Plus ne suit ce qui j'ay esté,
> Et ne le scaurois jamais estre.
> Mon beau printemps et mon esté
> Ont fait le sault par le fenestre.
> Amour tu as esté mon maistre,
> Je t'ay servi sur tous les Dieux.
> O si je pouvois deux fois naistre,
> Comme je te servirois mieux.

The merit of this so much depends on the delicacy and happy turn of the expression that I am loth to venture it in English.

Clement Marot, whom I have thus endeavoured to introduce to the notice of my readers, was born at Cahors, in Quercy, in 1484. His father, Jean,* a Norman, was also a poet of some celebrity ; as appears from an epigram addressed by his son to Hugues Salel, another writer of whom it is intended to give some account in a future paper.

* Jean Marot's poems were published at Paris, 1723, in two volumes ; together with those of Michel, who was, I think, the son of Clement.

> De Jan de Meun s'enfle le cours de Loire.
> En maistre Alain Normandie prent gloire :
> Et plaint encore mon arbre paternel.

" The Loire swells with pride at the name of Jean de Meun. Normandy glories in Master Alain (Alain Chartier), and still mourns for my paternal tree."

During the captivity of Francis I in Spain, Clement was apprehended on a suspicion of heresy, and confined in the Châtelet at Paris, from whence he was transferred to Chartres. Having been delivered through the intercession of his friends, but still fearing a second imprisonment, he took refuge, first with Margaret of Navarre, the King's sister, and afterwards at Ferrara, with Renée, Duchess of that city and daughter of Louis XII. To these events in his life he refers in some verses addressed to those through whose kindness he had obtained his freedom.

> J'euz à Paris prison fort inhumaine :
> A Chartres fuz doucement encloué :
> Maintenant vois, ou mon plaisir me maine ;
> C'est bien et mal. Dieu soit de tout loué.

" At Paris my prison was a cruel one ; in my confinement at Chartres I had milder usage. Now I go where my pleasure leads me. It is good and evil. God be praised for all."

At Ferrara, he contracted a friendship with Calvin, and is said to have embraced the opinions of that reformer. But, at the solicitation of Paul III, the Duke of

Ferrara determined on banishing all the wits and learned men, who were suspected of heresy, out of his territories ; and the Duchess prevailed on the King of France to allow Marot to return to his court, and to restore him to favour, on condition of his again becoming a dutiful son of the Church. Against the charge of dissension he thus defends himself :

" I am neither Lutheran nor Zuinglian ; and still less an Anabaptist : I am of God by His Son Jesus Christ. I am one that have written many a poem ; from none of which a single line can be adduced contrary to the divine law. I am one whose whole delight and labour it is to exalt my Saviour and his all-gracious Mother. The best proof of this may be found in my writings."

From his verses to the King, written during his residence at Ferrara, it appears that he thought himself in danger of being put to the stake as a heretic. The argument which he uses to defend himself on account of having prohibited books in his possession are much the same as Milton has since urged on a similar subject in his Areopagitica.

On his return to France in 1536, he employed himself in translating some of the Psalms into French metre, from the version of Vatable, the royal professor of Hebrew, which gave so much scandal to the doctors of the Sorbonne that they induced the King to prevent him from continuing his work.

Still, however, he persisted in delivering his sentiments on religion with such freedom as to keep alive the resentment of his enemies ; and he at last found it necessary to remove to Geneva. Here he was accused of having committed some gross irregularities of conduct, of which I am willing to believe him innocent. He then retired to Turin, and died in poverty at the age of sixty.

THIBAUT,
KING OF NAVARRE*

1201-1253

———

WHETHER Thibaut, King of Navarre, was or was not the favoured lover of Blanch, Queen Regent of France and mother of Louis the Ninth, is a question that has been much debated. Those who maintain the affirmative rely chiefly on the hearsay evidence of Mathew Paris, and on the assertion of an old French chronicler, whose name and age are unknown. On the other side are to be taken into the account the total silence of Joinville, the contemporary historian on the subject, and that of several other annalists who lived at or near the time, the general good character of Blanch, and the disparity of her years, for she was nearly old enough to be the mother of Thibaut. But a scandalous report, however improbable, when it has been once broached, seldom fails to spread far and wide ; and the " Fama refert " of Mathew has been eagerly caught at by a host of later writers,

———

* This notice of Thibaut, as it carries us back to an earlier period than any of the after pages, so was it written and published prior to all the rest. It is, however, placed second in this volume because the account of Clement Marot purports to introduce us to the series.—**Ed.**

amongst whom are Duhaillan, the first of French historians, who incorporated the annals of his country into the narration; Favin, who wrote the history of Navarre; Mezerai; Rapin; and the Père Daniel.

It is well known that the curtailment of one word, which a hasty scribe had reduced to the unlucky consonants *prtbus*, has thrown the whole life and character of Petrarch's Laura into confusion and perplexity. Did he mean it for *parturitionibus*? He did, says that Abbé de Sade, at the same time claiming for himself the honour to derive his parentage from one of these ill-omened throes; and immediately the modest nymph of the Sorga is transformed into a married coquette, with as large a litter about her as the boon goddess in Mr. Hilton's picture has, and the little biographer straining after his own bubble at the top. Shall we substitute *perturbationibus* with Lord Woodhouselee? It is quite another story: Laura is not only reinstated in her " single blessedness " but is rendered an object of interest and compassion by her numerous and undeserved sufferings.

Something of the same sort has happened in the case we are now considering. In the first of his songs, according to one of the manuscripts in the Royal Library at Paris,* the King of Navarre calls his mistress " La blonde couronnée "—" The crowned fair." " On reading this," says the editor of the Chansons† (to whose account of the matter I am indebted for my information), " I had no doubt but that Thibaut was enamoured of

* No. 7222.

† Les Poesies du Roy de Navarre, avec des Notes et un Glossaire Francois, &c. Paris, 1742. 2 tom. 8vo.

Blanch." But the inadvertence of a transcriber had again thrown an unmerited suspicion on the innocent. On consulting other written copies of the same song, the candid enquirer owned that he had discovered reasons for altering his mind. In them, " La blonde colorée "* were the words, which, in Shakespeare's language, may be rendered, one—

> Whose red and white,
> Nature's own sweet and cunning hand laid on.

and the character of the Queen was again cleared.

It is quite lamentable to think how slight an accident may destroy or impeach the reputation of a virtuous princess in the eyes of posterity. I could wish that the old Punic language were recovered, and that some Carthaginian manuscripts could be disinterred which should equally rescue the fame of Dido from the aspersions cast upon it by Virgil, who, it is to be feared, though a modest man on the whole, was yet, as a determined bachelor, somewhat free in his opinions on certain points, and besides much corrupted by his intimacy with Horace. The vindication which Ercilla, the heroic poet of Spain (in this instance so truly deserving of the title), has undertaken of her cause might be triumphantly established.

Without thus clearing the way, I could not have reconciled it to myself to say a word about the Chansons of Thibaut. But having so far satisfied my conscience,

---

* The same combination of words occurs elsewhere in these songs, and in the Romant de la Rose :
> La face blanche colorée,
> L'haleine douce et savourée.

of which I hold it the duty of every critic on such occasions to be very tender, I have the less scruple in laying before my readers an imitation of one of these songs.

First, however, I shall premise a few remarks on the origin and nature of French song-writing, which I have gleaned out of a learned dissertation by the editor before mentioned.

It appears that abusive ballads (the first species of songs that are known to have been composed in that language) were made as early as the expedition of Godfrey of Bouillon, on the occasion of Arnulf, chaplain to the Count of Normandy, being appointed Patriarch of Jerusalem, after he had disgraced himself by some irregularities of conduct during his march to the holy city. Gautier de Coincy, a monk of St. Medard de Soissons, composed a large number of songs, yet remaining in manuscript together with his other poems. He was in the time of Philip Augustus. The next to Coincy were those writers of songs contained in the manuscripts of which the King of Navarre's form a part. Of these, Chrétien de Troyes and Aubion de Sezane wrote at the end of the twelfth century. Thibaut, King of Navarre, who was born in 1201, and died in 1253, is said to have been distinguished from the rest not more by his high station than by the superior elegance and refinement of his style.

The first French songs were called Lais, from the Latin *lessus*, a complaint ; though they had often no more pretensions to the name than the nightingale has to the title of the " melancholy bird." Like the Provençal, they have in general five stanzas, with an envoi at the end. The measure is most commonly the ten-syllable, with a pause on the fourth. The rhymes are very exact, not only to the eye, but to the ear ; but an indispensable alteration of the masculine and feminine rhymes was not adopted till the age of Marot and Ronsard ; though one or two instances of it may be found in Thibaut's songs.

The following is one that was composed by him as an encouragement to the Crusaders. I had intended to entertain my readers with one of his love ditties ; but the subject of this was so much more uncommon, and it seemed to bear so strongly the marks of a deep and solemn feeling, that I have selected it in preference to the rest. Thibaut was not one of those " who reck not their own rede," for he himself served in the holy wars ; and it might be for this, amongst his other worthy deeds, that the great Italian poet, who was very near his time, has given him the name of the " buon rè Tebaldo,"* the " Good King Thibault." It may be supposed to have been written about the year 1236, at the time when he joined the Crusaders.

Take him, O Lord, who to that land shall go,
 Where he did die and live who reigns with Thee :
But scarce shall they the road to heaven know
 Who will not bear His cross beyond the sea.
By such as have compassion and kind thought
Of their dear Lord, His vengeance should be sought,
 And freedom for his land and his countrie.

* Dante's Inferno, c. xxii.

But yonder all the evil men will stay,
   Who love not God, nor truth, nor loyalty.
" What will betide my wife ? " shall each one say ;
   " I would not leave my friends for any fee."
Fond is the trust wherein they put their stead ;
For friend is none, save Him that without dread
   Did hang for us upon the holy tree.

Now on shall go each valiant knight and squire
   That loves his God, and holds his honour dear,
And wisely doth the bliss of heaven desire.
   But drivellers, skulking at their hearths for fear,
Keep far away : such deem I blind indeed,
That succour not their God when He hath need,
   And for so little lose their glory here.

God, who for us did suffer on the tree,
   To all their doom in that great day shall tell :
" Ye, who have help'd to bear the rood for me,
   Ye to that place shall go where angels dwell,
Me there to view, and mine own Mother Maid :
But ye, by whom I had not ever aid,
   Down shall ye sink into the deep of hell."

Whoso in weal would pass their life away,
   Nor meet at all with trouble or affright,
They are his foes esteem'd ; such sinners they,
   As have nor sense, nor hardihood, nor might.
Our hearts, good Lord, from such vain thoughts set free,
And lead us to Thy land so holily,
   That we may stand before Thy blessed sight.

The Envoi.

Sweet lady, crowned queen above,
Pray for us, Virgin, in thy love ;
So shall we guide henceforth our steps aright.

ANTOINE HEROET

d. 1568

ANTOINE HEROET, how strange soever his name may now appear, in his own day was thought worthy of being put in competition with Clement Marot, who has had the better fortune of being still at least talked of. Joachim du Bellay, in his Defence and Illustration of the French Language, in which he has spoken of both more than once, informs us of the qualities by which each of them had attracted his own particular set of admirers. One man, says he, will tell you that he likes Marot, because he is easy, and not far removed from the matter of common discourse; another, that Heroet pleases him, because his verses are learned, grave and elaborate. It has happened as might be expected—the natural vein of the one has outlasted the erudition of the other.

Heroet may properly be called a metaphysical poet. Johnson, with some latitude of expression, has given that name to Cowley and some of the other wits in Charles the Second's time, and, with still less propriety, has considered those writers to be followers of Marino, who is very lavish in his descriptions, and much disposed, in Ovid's manner, to play upon his words, but not at all metaphysical : for it is possible that a writer may be highly metaphysical, and yet free from conceits ; as he may be full of conceits and yet not in the least open to the charge of being metaphysical.

La Parfaite Amie, The Perfect Mistress, the first poem in Heroet's collection, is in a strain of excessive Platonic refinement throughout. But he has clothed his abstruse conceptions in language that is utterly devoid of affectation, and, besides, nearer to that of the present day than Marot's. I have selected an allegorical story* out of the second book, which, however mysterious the allusion in it may be, is yet, for the cleanness of the expression (if I may be allowed such a phrase), comparable to some of the choice passages in our dramatic writers of Elizabeth's age.

> There is an isle
> Full, as they say, of good things, fruits and trees
> And pleasant verdure : a very masterpiece
> Of Nature's ; there the men immortally
> Live, following all delights and pleasures. There
> Is not, nor ever hath been, winter's cold
> Or summer's heat : the season still the same,
> One gracious spring, where all, e'en the worst used
> By Fortune, are content. Earth willingly
> Pours out her blessing : the words " thine " and
>   " mine "
> Are not known 'mongst them : all is common, free

* This story is also in Bembo, Gli Asolani, fol. 99, ed. Ven. 1546.

From pain and jealous grudging.   Reason rules,
Not Fantasy : that everyone knows well
What he would ask of other ; everyone,
What to command : thus everyone hath that
Which he doth ask ; what is commanded, does.

   This island hath the name of Fortunate ;
And, as they tell, is govern'd by a Queen
Well spoken, and discreet, and therewithal
So beautiful that, with one single beam
Of her great beauty, all the country round
Is render'd shining.   When she sees arrive
(As there are many so exceeding curious
They have no fear of danger 'fore their eyes)
Those who come suing to her, and aspire
After the happiness which she to each
Doth promise in her city, she doth make
The strangers come together ; and forthwith,
Ere she consenteth to retain them there,
Sends for a certain season all to sleep.

   When they have slept so much as there is need,
Then wake they them again ; and summon them
Into her presence.   There avails them not
Excuse or caution ; speech, however bland,
Or importunity of cries.   Each bears
That on his forehead written visibly
Whereof he hath been dreaming. They, whose dreams
Have been of birds and hounds, are straight dismiss'd ;
And, at her royal mandate, led away,
To dwell thenceforward with such beasts as these.
He who hath dream'd of sconces broken, war,
And turmoils, and seditions, glory won,
And highest feats achieved, is, in like guise,

An exile from her court ; whilst one, whose brow
Is pale and dead, and wither'd, showing care
Of pelf and riches, she no less denies
To be his queen and mistress.   None, in brief,
Reserves she of the dreamers in her isle,
Save him, that, when awaken'd he returns,
Betrayeth tokens that, of her rare beauty,
His dreams have been.   So great delight has she,
In being and in seeming beautiful,
Such dreamer is right welcome to her isle.
   All this is held a fable ; but who first
Made and recited it hath in this fable
Shadowed a truth.

Another passage, in the third book of this poem, is
curious, as it shows what the prevalent taste in female
beauty was at that time.

   Love is not such a strange enchanter
   That he can change a black eye to a hazel,
   Or turn dark brown into a pearly white,
   Or shape a grosser feature into fineness.
   And yet, when seated in a gentle heart,
   So subtle and so piercing is his fire
   He makes a woman's body all transparent ;
   And, in her visage, doth present to view
   I know not what, that words cannot express,
   Which makes itself be more, than beauty, loved.

This is one of the many instances in which the early
French poets have spoken of the " yeux verds," " green
eyes " (which I have taken the liberty of translating

into hazel), as being admired above all others. So we
find in Romeo and Juliet, Act iii, sc. 5.

> An eagle, madam,
> Hath not so green, so quick, so fair an eye.

The next poem by Heroet is formed on the fiction,
in Plato's Banquet, of the Androgynon : a poetical
epistle to Francis I is prefixed to it.

His other pieces are much in the same style.

I have learnt nothing more concerning this writer
than that he was made Bishop of Digne by Francis I ;
that he was, nevertheless, like Marot, suspected of
Calvinism, and that he died in the year 1568.

In this same volume (which, by the way, is printed
in a running type of uncommon neatness, and is in
De Bure's Bibliographie), at p. 237, is a poem entitled,
Nouvel Amour, which I find, by a manuscript note,
to be by the Sieur Papillon, though the writer of the note
must be mistaken in saying (as he does) that it is extracted
from a similar book, printed at Paris, 1551, in 16mo,
as that date is posterior to the date of the present
volume.

There is a fine description in it of the trouble throughout all nature, as a quarrel between Venus and her son.
It ends thus :

> Earth with a dismal scream was severed ;
> And gathering darkness o'er her visage spread.
> Upon the tops of towers the fays were seen
> To trail long robes of gold and silver sheen ;
> And mutter'd, as they pass'd, their uncouth wonder,
> Fearing the firmament should fall asunder.

And thrice was heard, in that ill-omen'd day,
A sound, that might the stoutest heart affray,
Of heavy hammers, clanking chains, and bars,
That mix'd in deepest hell their horrid jars.

The dispute is settled by the intervention of Jupiter.
At p. 269 there follows a letter in rhyme, called Le
Discours de Voyage de Constantinople, envoyé dudit
lieu à une Damoyselle de France, par le Seigneur de
Borderie.

" An Account of a Voyage to Constantinople, sent
from the said place to a young French Lady, by the
Seigneur de Borderie." On their way, among other
places, they touch at Athens.

" We had not half a day's leisure allowed us to see this
place, where we were much delighted, beholding the
foundations of the noble city entire, and covered with
grass. Their extensive traces sufficiently marked the
great space which it has comprised. We perceived also
a theatre, which length of time had not been able to
demolish, upon great pillars of marble, handsomely
placed, sixteen lengthwise, and, in front, six by six.
The Greeks, after their fashion, had made of it a church,
dedicated to Saint Andrew; having a round wall within,
manifestly of modern construction."

The remainder is, for the most part, equally humble
with this extract.

MELLIN DE SAINT GELAIS

1491—1559

———

MELLIN DE SAINT GELAIS is commended by Joachim du Bellay, in that poet's address to the reader prefixed to his own works, for having been the first who distinguished himself as a writer of sonnets in the French language. He left only seventeen of them. At least, I find no more in the collection of his poems, published soon after his decease. But it was a prolific race, and in a short time multiplied exceedingly.

Two out of these seventeen will, I daresay, satisfy the reader as to quantity. And, for the quality, I can assure him they are not the worst of the batch.

So many barques are not for Venice bound ;
 Nor oysters, Bourg can show, or calves Bretagne ;
 Or Savoy, bears ; or leverets, Champagne ;
 Or Thamis, silver swans, his shores around :
Not amorous treaties so at church abound,
 Or quarrels in the Diet of Almaine,
 Not so much boasting in a Don of Spain,
 Not so much feigning at the Court is found :

Monsters so numerous hath not Africa,
  Nor minds so various a republic bred,
  Nor pardons are at Rome on holyday,
Or cravings underneath a lawyer's gown,
  Or reas'nings with the doctors of Sorbonne :
As there are lunes in my sweet lady's head.

ON THE DAUPHIN

Thou, who art second in our noble France,
  Mayst cull at will, along each blooming mead,
  These pinks, whose hues for thee alone are spread,
  First opening with the morning's early glance ;
For thee the rose-bush doth his top advance,
  Whose coronals, with buttons vermeil-red,
  Blush all for shame to hold so high their head,
  Trusting yet more thy pleasure to enhance.
The milk-white Galathea, lily-crown'd,
  For thee in panniers twain her fruits doth screen,
  One veil'd with olive, one with myrtle green.
Thus sang fair Ægle, while the nymphs around
  Smiled as they listen'd ; and Pan heard the song,
  And to great Harry bade the notes belong.

The Sonnet was not the only form of composition adopted by Saint Gelais from the Italian tongue. He borrowed from it the Ottava Rima also.

In the Chant Villanesque (p. 235) he has counterfeited the charm of a rustic simplicity with much skill.

Mellin was supposed to be the natural son of Octavien de Saint Gelais, Sieur de Lunsac, and Bishop of Angoulême, and was born in 1491. The father, besides his own original works, among which the Vergier d'Honneur was one, was the author of translations into French verse of the Æneid, several books of the Odyssey, and the Epistles and Ars Amandi of Ovid. His profession did not restrain him from much freedom both in his life and writings. He is said to have bestowed great pains on his son's education, who profited as well as could be hoped under such a guide and tutor ; for he learnt to write verses better than his father, but with a sufficient portion of ribaldry in them. Mellin had a high reputation in the courts of Francis I and Henry II. He was Abbot of Recluz, and royal almoner and librarian.

A copy of verses directed to Clement Marot (p. 176), when they were both in ill-health, shows his regard for that poet. It begins :

" Glory and regret of the Poets of France, Clement Marot ; thy friend Saint Gelais, who is as much grieved by thy long suffering as he is charmed by thy songs and lays, etc."

Both he and Clement celebrated the restoration of Laura's tomb, at Avignoon, by Francis I.

He addresses also Hugues Salel, of whom we shall soon hear more ; though they had not yet made an acquaintance with each other.

His conduct towards Ronsard was somewhat ungenerous ; but that poet, with his characteristic generosity, forgave more than once the ill offices which Saint Gelais was supposed to have done him in court.

His talent for epigrammatic satire was so much dreaded that " Gare à la tenaille de Saint Gelais," " 'Ware of Saint Gelais pincers," became a proverbial saying.

He was celebrated for his skill in Latin poetry, and composed the following verses, when near his end.

Barbite, qui varios lenisti pectoris æstus,
Dum juvenem nunc sors, nunc agitabat amor ;
Perfice ad extremum, rapidæque incendia febris
Qua potes infirmo fac leviora seni.
Certe ego te faciam, superas evectus ad auras,
Insignem ad Cytharæ sidus habere locum.

Harp, that didst soothe my cares when opening life
With love and fortune waged alternate strife,
Fulfil thy task : allay the fervid rage
Of fever preying on my feeble age :
So, when I reach the skies, a place shall be,
Near the celestial lyre, allotted thee.

He died in Paris, in 1559. His works were re-edited, with additions, in that city, 1719 ; as I find in De Bure's Bibliographia.

HUGUES SALEL

1508—1558

H UGUES SALEL is one of those writers
who, having been much caressed and
applauded by their contemporaries, meet
with a different treatment from posterity. Looking
into a modern compilation of some authority for an
account of him, I find that he is pronounced to be awk-
ward, embarrassed, and languid ; and that he is without
any ceremony condemned to a place among the poets
that merit no better fate than to lie on the shelf, and be
gnawn by worms. I suppose, therefore, that it is in this
vermicular capacity I must own that I have tasted, and
found him no unsavoury food.

If matters come to the worst, there is something
at least in his title-page that will be relished by all those
who honour an old book, as some honour a great man,
for nothing else but the title. Here is the style in which
it runs :—" Les Œuvres de Hugues Salel, Valet de
Chambre ordinaire du Roy, imprimees par Commande-
ment dudict Seigneur. Avec Privilege pour six Ans.
Imprimé à Paris, pour Estienne Roffet, dit le Faulcheur,
Relieur du Roy, et Libraire en ceste Ville de Paris, de-
mourant sur le Pont S. Michel, à Lanseigne de la Roze
blanche."—" The Works of Hugues Salel, Valet de

Chambre in ordinary to the King. Imprinted by Commandment of the said Lord. With Privilege for six Years. Imprinted at Paris, by Stephen Roffet, called the Mower, Binder to the King, and Bookseller in this Town of Paris, abiding on the Bridge Saint Michael, at the Sign of the White Rose." There is no date except in manuscript at the bottom of the page, which imports it to have been printed in the year 1539. Whoever wishes to preserve his character as a bibliomaniac (so they have termed it of late years) will go no further than this. They who can pluck up a good courage, and are not afraid of the more odious name to which they may subject themselves by pursuing the quest, will venture onwards. The first poem then, or the first play for the worms, whichsoever we shall term it, in this collection is a " Royal Chase, that containeth the taking of the Wild Boar Discord, by the very high and very potent Princes, the Emperor Charles the Fifth, and the King Francis, the First of this Name."—" Chasse Royalle, contenant la prise du Sanglier Discord, par tres haultz et tres puissans Princes, l'Empereur Charles Cinquiesme, et le Roy François, premier de ce Nom." France and Spain being in a state of perfect peace and happiness, all the Gods receive due homage from mortals, except Mars ; who, enraged at the neglect, descends to the lower regions, and brings up the wild boar Discord to earth. Charles V and Francis I unite to hunt down the monster, whose defeat, with the help of other European princes, they soon accomplish. This is a slight sketch, and somewhat pedantic ; but I should say that it was filled up with much spirit.

In the Marin Eclogue on the death of the Dauphin

François de Valois, there are some verses of remarkable sweetness, which remind me of Lydgate.

The Punishment of Cupid is another poem in which the materials, though very slender, are wrought up with a certain portion of elegance and fancy.

The following song may be considered as a testimony on the long-pending suit with respect to the song of the Nightingale.

> Ye nightingales, whose voice divine
>> Thrills out these greenwood glades among,
> Oh ! fill no more those ears of mine.
>> With such a sweet and pleasant song.
> Ye see the way I now am wending,
>> Unto a place whence joy is flown ;
> Then but for once a sad note lending,
>> Sing, an ye will, my mistress gone.

Like most of his brethren, he celebrates the " green eyes " of his mistress :

> Marguerite aux yeulx rians et verds. (F. 53.)

The " laughing eye " would be too bold an expression for a Frenchman nowadays ; and accordingly one of them, who met with it in translating Dante—

> Ond'ella pronta e con occhi ridenti. (Par. C. 3.)

has translated it—

> L'ombre me repondit d'un air satisfait.

There are some more poems by Salel, printed at the end of the " Amours d'Olivier de Magny," of which I shall speak presently. The most remarkable amongst them are three Chapitres d'Amour (as they are called), in which he uses the Italian measure called the Terza Rima. It was adopted by some of our writers in Henry VIII and Elizabeth's time, as Sir Thomas Wyatt, Sir Frs. Bryan, Sir Philip Sydney; and afterwards by Milton, in his version of the second Psalm. Yet Mr. Hayley supposed that he was the first to introduce it into our language, in that spirited translation of the first three cantos of Dante which he inserted in the notes to his Essay on Epic Poetry; and Lord Byron, when he adopted it in a late poem called the Vision of Dante, was not aware of Mr. Hayley's mistake.

At the command of Francis I, Salel undertook to translate the Iliad, but did not proceed further than the beginning of the thirteenth book. By a preface to the eleventh and twelfth books, and a fragment of the thirteenth, edited after his death by Olivier de Magny, it seems he was accused of having made use of a Latin version instead of the original Greek. " But I was his amanuensis," adds Magny, " and can with truth bear witness to the contrary." Whether it was made from the Latin or the Greek, his translation is but a lame one. It is curious to see how he has contrived to strip the moonlight landscape at the end of the eighth book of more than half its splendour.

> Et tout ainsi que l'on peult voir souvent,
> En temps serain, prés de la lune claire,
> Les corps du ciel (car ung chascun esclaire
> Tant que les montz, les vallées et plaines
> Sont de lumiere ainsi qu'en beau jour pleines).
> Dont le berger que sa veuë en haut jette,
> Se resjouit en sa basse logette.

But there is another extreme. All my readers remember Pope's version of this :

As when the moon, resplendent lamp of night, etc.

and, if they have not yet seen Mr. Coleridge's observations upon it in his Bibliographia Literaria, Vol. I, p. 39, I would recommend them to their notice.

In another famous simile, that in the fifth book, of the clouds amassed on the mountain tops by Jove, his anxiety that all should be well understood has caused him to make strange work of these cumulo-strati.

> Ainsi que les nues
> Sont bien souvent sur les montz retenuës
> Maulgré les ventz, par le dieu Jupiter,
> Que ne pourroient aultrement resister
> Au soufflement, et tourbillon divers
> Du vent de nort qui leur donne à travers ;
> Semblablement, etc.

But this is quite enough of his Homer.

Hugues Salel, of Casalé, in Querci, was born about the year 1508.

> Quercy, Salel, de toi se vantera ;
> Et (comme croy) de moi ne se taira.

are Marot's words to him in the Epigram on the French poets, to which I have referred in the account of that writer.

" Querci will boast itself in thee, Salel ; and, as I think, will not pass my name in silence."

Ronsard esteemed him one of the first who began to write well in France.

Besides the other marks of favour which he received from the open-hearted Francis I he was presented by that monarch with the abbey of Saint Cheron, near Chartres ; where he died in the year 1558.*

* Salel's birth is dated about 1504, his death in 1553, by the editor of "Choix des Poésies de P. de Ronsard, &c." 12mo. Par. 1826, p. 79.

OLIVIER DE MAGNY

d. 1560

THE first production I have met with from the pen of Olivier de Magny is entitled Les Amours d'Olivier de Magny, Quercinois, et quelques Odes de lui. Ensemble un recueil d'aucunes Œuvres de Monsieur Salel, Abbé de Saint Cheron, non encore veuës. A Paris. Vincent Sartenan, 1553, 8vo. In this collection, Magny's sonnets (in the common or ten-syllable measure) are in the taste of the Italian Petrarchisti, or imitators of Petrarch. In some of the odes there is more nature. That on a nosegay presented to him by Castianira (F. 56) has a peculiar vivacity and richness, and is very much in Ben Jonson's way.

His next work is Les Gayetez d'Olivier de Magny à Pierre Paschal, Gentilhomme du Bas Pais de Languedoc,

> Non tamen est facinus molles evolvere versus,
>   Multa licet caste non facienda legant.

A Paris, pour Jean Dallier, 1554, 8vo.

There is much ease in these trifles. If I were to select one of the most pleasing, it would be that to Corydon, Ronsard's servant, which gives an engaging picture of that poet's manner of life.

And if he with his troop repair
   Sometimes into the fields,
Seek thou the village nigh, and there
   Choose the best wine it yields.
Then by a fountain's mossy side,
   O'er which some hawthorn bends,
Be the full flask by thee supplied
   To cheer him and his friends.

We shall be reminded of the hawthorn when we come to Ronsard himself. These poets seem to have enjoyed nature with an unceremonious gaiety and frankness of heart not known to their successors in the days of Louis XIV.

The last publication, I have seen, of Olivier de Magny, is called Les Soupirs. Paris. Par Jean Dallier, 1557. 8vo.

These Sighs vent themselves in a hundred and seventy-six sonnets, some of which, fortunately, are anything but dolorous; as may be seen by the following:

Up; sweep the papers off; the table clear:
   I will no more of these, good boy, to-day.
   All trouble shall be held awhile at bay,
   And naught but mirth and pleasure shall come near.
For see, my friend, my dearest Cassin here:
   This is a festal and no working day:
   Bid each intruder hence; we will be gay
   Together, and alone make joyous cheer,
I will with Love himself a brief truce keep:
   I will with white chalk score this day for gladness;
   I will to Bacchus only homage pay;
Yea, I will laugh and leap and dance away,
   And drain at last the brimming bowl so deep
   I care not if it end in merry madness.

It has been observed by Johnson that in Milton's mirth there is some melancholy. In Magny's melancholy there is certainly much mirth. He does not seem to have been made for sighing. Yet it might have been enough to make him do so if he could have known that in so short a time his countrymen would no longer think him worthy of a place in their voluminous works of biography.* This must be my excuse for having nothing to tell either of his birth, his fortunes, or his decease. He was of Querci. His verses bespeak him to have been a good soul, free from envy and ill-nature ; and he was prized accordingly by the wits of his age Be this his record.

* There is a notice of Olivier de Magny in the " Choix des Poésies de P. de Ronsard," &c. 12mo. Par. 1826, p. 136.

JOACHIM DU BELLAY

1524—1560

Bellay ! first garland of free poesy
That France brought forth, though fruitful of brave
    wits ;
Well worthy thou of immortality,
That long has travel'd by thy learned writs,
Old Rome out of her ashes to revive,
And give a second life to dead decays ;
Needs must he all eternity survive,
That can to others give eternal days.
Thy days, therefore, are endless ; and thy praise
Excelling all that ever went before.

SUCH is the encomium which Spenser annexes
to his translation of The Ruines of Rome,
by Bellay. It is somewhat too lofty for the
occasion ; and is made of less value by being coupled
with the praise of Bartas, whose Muse has not much
right to the epithet bestowed on her in the ensuing lines,
except it be for the subject of which she treats.

And after thee 'gins Bartas hie to raise
His heavenly Muse, th' Almighty to adore.
Live, happy spirits ! th' honour of your name,
And fill the world with never dying fame.

Yet this honourable testimony from the author of the Faery Queene, who has still more distinguished the subject of it by translating several of his poems, secures for Joachim du Bellay undeniable claims to attention and deference from an English reader. When, indeed, we consider, that not only the boast of Eliza's days dipped his plumes in the Gallic Hippocrene, but that the Father of English poetry used to refresh himself largely at the same fountain, we cannot look upon it but as a source of hallowed waters.

In the Defence and Illustration of the French Language,* a judicious and well-written treatise, to which I have more than once had occasion to refer, Bellay betrays a want of reverence for his predecessors which has been amply retaliated by posterity of his own age. Of all the ancient French poets, he observes that Guillaume de Lorris and Jean de Meun are almost the only authors worth reading ; and that, not because there is much in them that deserves imitation, but for that first image, as it were, which they present of the French language, made venerable by its antiquity. He adds that the more recent were those named by Clement Marot, in his Epigram to Hugues Salel ; and that Jan le Maire de Belges seemed to him the first who had illustrated the French language ; by which he explains himself to mean that he imparted to it many poetical words and phrases, of which the most excellent writers of his own time had availed themselves.† Most of these, I doubt, have since been thrown away by the purist.

* Œuvres de Joachim du Bellay. Paris edition in 12mo, about 1568.

† L. ii. ch. 2.

He speaks of " vers libres," unfettered verse ; such, he says, as had been used by Petrarch, and by Luigi Alamanni in his not less learned than pleasant poem on Agriculture.* Alamanni, indeed, who during his retreat from Florence had experienced the liberality and protection of Francis I and who was probably known to Bellay at the court of that monarch, had written his Coltivazione in blank verse ; and some, though without sufficient ground for the assertion, have pronounced him to be the first who employed it in a long poem. But that Petrarch ever wrote Italian poetry without rhyme, or that he ever mingled versi sciolti, or blank verse, in his compositions, as Boccaccio is observed to have done, I am not aware that any other critic has asserted.

While I am on this subject let me remark that it is to the Italians we owe our blank verse ; and that the two books of the Æneid, in the translating of which it is believed to have been first introduced amongst us by Surrey, were about the same time translated into Italian blank verse ; the second book by the Cardinal Ippolito de Medici, and the fourth by Lodovico Martelli.

Bellay would not have the alternation of male and female rhymes too strictly adhered to. This was a meritorious though unsuccessful attempt to deliver the French verse from one of its most galling fetters.† Like Ronsard, he advises the frequenting persons of all different handicrafts, in order to collect terms, and to deduce comparisons and descriptions.‡

* L. ii. ch. 7.
† Œuvres de Joachim du Bellay. Paris edition in 12mo, about 1588 ; ch. 9.
‡ Ibid. ch. 11.

Amongst the French writers are adduced by way of distinction Guillaume Budé and Lazare de Baïf, the latter of whom had translated the Electra of Sophocles, almost line for line, " quasi vers par vers."[*]

But to come to his poems. His Olive is a collection of one hundred and fifteen sonnets, nearly all of them, excepting a few of the last, on the subject of his love, which he shadows forth under the figure of that tree, as Petrarch had done his under that of a laurel. The word itself is an anagram of Viole, the real name of the lady whom he celebrates, and who was an inhabitant of Angers. In the twenty-eighth is found the sentiment in a common but very pretty French song, which the unfortunate Major André was fond of applying to his Honora. I write it from memory, having never seen it in print :

> Ah ! si vous pouviez comprendre
>   Ce que je ressens pour vous ;
> L'amour n'a rien de si tendre,
>   Ni l'amitié de si doux.
> Loin de vous mon cœur soupire,
>   Près de vous suis interdit :
> Voilà tout ce que j'ose dire,
>   Et peutêtre j'ai trop dit.

Bellay has it :

> Ce que je sens, la langue ne refuse
> Vous descouvrir quand suis de vous absent ;
> Mais tout soudain que pres de moy vous sent,
> Elle devient et muette et confuse.

We have, I believe, an English song in which the

same natural feeling is expressed ; but I am not able to recollect the words of it.

The sixtieth sonnet is to Ronsard, whom he has addressed in several of his poems. When we come to that poet, we shall again have occasion to admire the nobleness of his mind, as displayed in his conduct towards Bellay.

The ninety-first is on the same subject as an Italian one by Bernardino Tomitano, a physician and public professor of logic at Padua ; he died a few years later than Bellay (in 1576). It is, therefore, not easy to say which of the two has the merit of being original ; perhaps neither of them—but the Frenchman's production has, I think, more the air of a copy.

> Yield to the spheres thy witching strain*
>   That from their orbs has roll'd
> To eastern climes, return again
>   Their fragrance, pearls, and gold.
> Be to the sun that brightness given
>   Thou borrow'st from this flame :
> And render back thy smile to heaven,
>   From whence its sweetness came.
> Owe to the morn thy blush no more,
>   Which from her cheek has flown.
> To seraph bands their truth restore,
>   Her chasteness to the moon.
> What then shall of those charms remain,
>   Which thou dost call thine own ;
> Except the pride and cold disdain
>   That turn thy slave to stone.

* This imitation of the above sonnet was not printed in the original article. The author has left a memorandum that it should be inserted.—ED.

There is one by Olivier de Magny on the same subject. It is the 172nd in his Soupirs, and begins :

Vos celestes beautés, dame, rendez aux cieux, etc.

For an English imitation, I must refer to the last volume of the *London Magazine* (1821), p. 411.
The ninety-sixth, which begins :

Ny par les bois les Dryades courantes,
Ny par les champs les fiers scadrons armés,
Ny par les flots les grands vaisseaux ramés, etc.

is certainly borrowed from an old Italian sonnet by Guido Cavalcanti, which is inserted, together with a version of it by a late translator of Dante, in his notes to the eleventh canto of the Purgatory.
Sonnet Ninety-seven, beginning—

Qui a peu voir la matinale rose,

is from Catullus and Ariosto, in passages too well known to be cited. Those in Sophocles—Trach. 144—and in Marino's Adone—C. xi. 62—are less obvious.
All the sonnets in the Olive are, I believe, in the " vers commun," the ten-syllable verse ; which is more agreeable to an English ear than the Alexandrine. The pause, as usual, is on the fourth syllable ; as is generally the case in our own Surrey. Of his other sonnets, there are some in each of these measures.
Not one of the old French poets that I have yet seen appears so much at home amongst the Italians, for whom, in the fourth ode of his Recueil, he testifies his warm admiration.

" What age shall extinguish the remembrance of thee, O Boccaccio ? and what hard winters, O Petrarch ! shall wither the glory of thy green laurels ? Who, Dante and Bembo, of proud and lofty spirit, shall see your memory fade ? "

Yet he laments most bitterly the engagements which compelled him to reside in Italy, and to put on a false appearance which he abhorred; and he longs to be again his own master, and to return to his own land. In the Regrets, where these feelings are expressed, there is much ease and nature. Some of the poems under that title exhibit lively pictures of the corruptions then prevalent in the several Italian courts, and especially at Rome. His talent for satire here shows itself. What in this way can exceed the following sonnet on Venice ?

It doth one good to see these Magnificoes,
  These proud poltroons ; their gorgeous arsenal ;
  Their roads o'erthrong'd with vessels ; their Saint
          Mark ;
  Their Palace ; their Rialto, and their Port ;
  Their Bank, their traffic ; their Exchange, their
          bart'ring :
  To see their antique hats with formal beak ;
  Their broad-sleeved mantles, and their unbrimm'd
          bonnets :
  It doth one good to mark their uncouth jabb'ring ;
  Their gravity ; their port ; their sage advice
  On public questions ; yea, it doth one good
  To see their senate balloting on each thing ;
  In every port their gondolas afloat ;

Their dames ; their masquing, and their lonely living.
But the best sight of all is to behold
When these old wittols go to wed the sea,
Whose spouses they are, and the Turk her leman.

The 151st sonnet, To Courtiers, is another that is
remarkable for its mixture of sprightliness, drollery,
and caustic humour.   England came in for a large portion
of his gall.   At F. 189 is a poem called Execration sur
l'Angleterre ; but in his Regrets (Sonnet 162) it appears
that he had been softened towards this country.

Of his Vœux Rustiques, imitated from the Latin of
Navagero, the following is no unfavourable specimen :

> D'un Vanneur de blé aux vents.
>
> A vous trouppe legere,
>> Qui d'aile passagere
>> Par le monde volez,
>> Et d'un sifflant murmure
>> L'ombrageuse verdure
>> Doucement esbranlez.
> J'offre ces violettes,
>> Ces lis et ces fleurettes,
>> Et ces roses icy
>> Ces vermeillettes roses,
>> Tout freschement éclauses,
>> Et ces œillets aussi.
> De vostre douce haleine
>> Evantez ceste pleine,
>> Evantez ce sejour :
>> Cependant que j'ahanne
>> A mon blé, que je vanne
>> A la chaleur du jour.   (F. 444.)

The original is in the taste of the Greek ἐπιγράμματα, of which no one knew the relish better than Navagero.

Auræ quæ levibus percurritis aëra pennis,
 Et strepitis blando per nemora alta sono ;
Serta dat hæc vobis, vobis hæc rusticus Idmon
 Spargit odorato plena canistra croco.
Vos lenite æstum, et paleas sejungite inanes,
 Dum medio fruges ventilat ille die.

This has been made a sonnet of by Lodovico Paterno ; and a fine one it is.

I wish I had something worthier to be put by the side of these than the attempt which is here offered to my reader.

Ye airs ! sweet airs, that through the naked sky
 Fan your aurelian wings in wanton play ;
Or shedding quiet slumber, as ye fly,
 'Mid the dim forest murmuring urge your way ;
To you these garlands, and this basket high
 Pil'd up with lily-bells and roses gay,
And fragrant violets of purplest dye,
 Icon, all fainting in the noontide ray,
Scatters, a votive offering to your power :
 And oh ! as ye receive the balmy spoil,
 Temper the inclement beam ; and while his flail
He plies unceasing through the sultry hour,
 Hoarse Echo answering ever to his toil,
 Dispel the parted chaff with brisker gale.

But to return to Bellay. His epitaphs on a little dog, on a cat, and on the Abbé Bonnet, are exquisitely droll and fantastic.

In his hyme De la Surdité, a whimsical encomium on Deafness, addressed to his friend Ronsard, there is some very striking imagery.

> Hail to thee, Deafness, boon and holy power,
> Thou that hast scoop'd thee out on ample bower
> Within a hard rock where thy throne is seen,
> Hung round with tapestry of mossy green,
> The stony tower, embattled, guards thy state,
> And Nile's steep falls are thundering at the gate.
> There Silence on thy right hand still doth sit,
> His finger on his lips ; and in a fit
> Of tranced sorrow, Melancholy lost,
> Upon thy left, life a for-pined ghost.
> A little lower, Study bends his look
> For ever glu'd upon his wide-spread book.
> Before thee, rapt Imagination stands,
> With brow to heaven uplifted, while her hands
> Present to thee a mirror of broad steel,
> That in its depth all wonders doth reveal,
> Of sky, and air, and earth, and the wide ocean ;
> All things that are, whether in rest or motion.
> Grave Judgment on thy lap in sleep profound
> Is laid ; and winged words flit hovering round.

His advice to the young king, Francis the Second, on his accession to the crown, is remarkable for its freedom. The poets of those times seem to have kept firm hold on one of the most valuable privileges of their profession, and not to have sunk the monitor in the courtier. Of the poems which Spenser translated from Bellay, the following Sonnet is rendered with a fidelity that has

not in the least injured its spirit. I have selected it
as the best of those which he has taken.

> On high hill's top I saw a stately frame,
>   An hundred cubits high by just assize,
> With hundred pillars fronting fair the same,
>   All wrought with diamond, after Dorick wise ;
> Nor brick nor marble was the wall to view,
>   But shining crystal, which from top to base
> Out of her womb a thousand rayons threw,
>   One hundred steps of Afric gold's enchase :
> Gold was the parget ; and the ceiling bright
>   Did shine all scaly, with great plates of gold ;
> The floor of jasp and emerald was dight.
>   Oh ! world's vainness ! whiles thus I did behold,
> An earthquake shook the hill from lowest seat,
> And overthrew this frame with ruine great.
>   (The Visions of Bellay, 2.)

Joachim du Bellay, descended from one of the noblest
families in Anjou, was born at Liré, a village eight miles
from Angers, in the year 1524.   The facility and sweetness with which he wrote gained him the appellation
of the French Ovid.   He was highly esteemed by Margaret of Valois, Queen of Navarre, and by Henry the
Second, who granted him a considerable pension.   He
passed some years in Italy, whither he went in the suite
of his kinsman, Cardinal du Bellay.   We have seen how
ill he was pleased with that country, and yet how much he
learned from it.   Another of his family, Eustache du
Bellay, Bishop of Paris, obtained for him in 1555 a canonry
in his church.   He was carried off at an early age by a

fit of apoplexy, in January, 1560, and was buried in the church of Notre Dame.

Many epitaphs were made for him, in which he was called Pater Elegantiarum ; Pater Omnium Leporum.

He wrote Latin poems that are not so much esteemed as his French.

REMY BELLEAU

1528—1577

———

THE Painter of Nature was the appellation
which distinguished Remy Belleau among
the poets of his time ; and it is enough
to obtain for him no ordinary share of regard
from those who know how much is implied in that
title, and how rare that merit is of which it may be considered as a pledge. I have not yet had the good fortune
to meet with an edition containing the whole of his
works. That which I have seen was printed during his
lifetime, with the following title : Les Amours et nou-
veaux Eschanges des Pierres precieuses ; Vertus et
Proprietez d'icelles. Discours de la Vanité, Pris de
l'Ecclesiaste. Eclogues Sacrées, Prises du Cantique des
Cantiques. Par Remy Belleau. A Paris par Mamert
Patisson, au logis de Rob. Estienne, 1576, avec privilege
du Roy. " The Loves and new Transformations of the
Precious Stones ; their Virtues and Properties. Discourse on Vanity, taken from Ecclesiastes. Sacred
Eclogues, taken from the Song of Songs, etc." There
is in these sufficient to prove that Belleau was not in
the habit of looking at nature through the eyes of other
men ; that he did not content himself with making
copies of copies ; but that he drew from the life when-
ever he had such objects to describe as the visible world

could supply him with.   Nor is this the whole of his praise ; for he has also some fancy, and a flow of numbers unusually melodious.

In the above collection, the first poem, on the Loves and Transformations of the Precious Stones, dedicated to Henry III, is on a plan not much more happy than that of Darwin's Loves of the Plants.   Several of them are supposed to have been youths or maidens, who, in consequence of adventures similar to those invented by the poet of the Metamorphoses, were changed into their present shape.   Thus, in the first of these tales, the nymph Amethyste, of whom Bacchus is enamoured, prays to Diana for succour, and by her is transformed into a stone, which the god dyes purple with the juice of the grape.   A description, which he has here introduced of the jolly god with the Bacchantes in different attitudes about his chariot, is executed with a luxuriance of pencil that reminds one of Rubens.

> A train of Mænads wanton'd round the car
> With light and frolic step ; one on the reins
> Hung of the ounces speckled o'er with stars,
> Of eye quick-glancing, and free supple foot,
> The long moustaches bristling from their maws :
> Another with quick hand the traces flung
> Across the tygers of the streaky skin :
> They yoked in pairs when snorting, and with ire
> Their restless eyeballs roll'd.   Fine cloth of gold,
> Sown o'er with pearls, hung mantling to their side,
> And at the knee the tassel'd fringes danced.
> Then, as their pride abated, in quaint curls
> They braid their wavy tails.

As a companion to this, I would place the fine picture
of Cybele's chariot drawn by lions, as Keats has painted
it.

> Forth from a rugged arch, in the dusk below,
> Came mother Cybele; alone, alone,
> In sombre chariot; dark foldings thrown
> About her majesty, and front death-pale,
> With turrets crown'd.   Four maned lions hale
> The sluggish wheels; solemn their toothed maws,
> Their surly eyes brow-hidden, heavy paws
> Uplifted drowsily, and nervy tails
> Cowering their tawny brushes.
>
> (Endymion, p. 83.)

In this pictorial manner there is an anonymous poem
of extraordinary merit, which, I believe, appeared first
in the *New Monthly Magazine*.   It is called the Indian
Circian.   The writer of it, whoever he may be, may well
aspire to the title of the Painter of Nature.

To return to Belleau.   Another of these little stories
is built on the fable of Hyacinthus, whose blood, when
he is killed by Apollo, forms the jacinth, at the same time
that the nymph Chrysolithe, who had requited his offered
love with scorn, poisons herself, and is changed into the
stone bearing her name.   The spot in which the
boy meets his fate, when he is playing at quoits with
Phœbus, is a piece of landscape-painting, sweetly
touched.

Iris being sent on one of her mistress's errands, stays
to refresh herself by the river Indus, where she sees and
becomes enamoured of Opalle:

Opalle, grand Berger des troupeaux de Neptune.
(F. 27.)
" Great Shepherd that on Neptune's flocks did
tend."

He is dazzled and overpowered by the advances of the
wind-footed goddess, and falls into a swoon ; but is
recovered out of it. Juno, meantime, being enraged
at the delay of her handmaid, goes in search of her, and
discovers them together. He is changed into a stone,
of which Iris makes the opal.

While Venus lies asleep, Love, fluttering about her,
sees her own image reflected on the polished surface of
her nails. He sets himself to carve out these mirrors
with the point of one of his darts, while she continues
in her slumber ; and then, flying off with them, he lets
them fall

" on the pearl'd sands
Of tawny Indus with the crisped locks."
. . . . . sur le sable perleux
De L'Indois basané sous ses crespes cheveux.

where they are changed into onyx-stones.

To these fanciful tales are appended directions for
distinguishing artificial stones from the true, together
with some remarks on their medical properties, and
their uses against incantations and sorceries. It scarcely
need be told how bad an effect so incongruous a mixture
produces. When Belleau made this addition, it is
probable that the Greek poem on Precious Stones,
which goes under the name of Orpheus, was in his
view.

In addressing the twelve chapters of his Discourse on Vanity, taken from Ecclesiastes, to Monseigneur (the Duke d'Alençon), he tells that prince that his brother (the late King, Charles IX) being at Fontaine-bleau was so much pleased with it that he had made him read over the first four chapters several times; that the King's death, and a grievous malady under which he had himself laboured, had interrupted his design; "but now being recovered," says he, "I present this work to you." This was in July, 1576. Having tuned the verses well, he has done nearly all that could be expected of him in this task. Much of the same may be said of the Sacred Eclogues, into which he has formed the Song of Songs. Profaner love employed his muse at another time; for he translated the poems attributed to Anacreon, which were then newly discovered, into French verse.

Among his other poems is the following Song on April: having seen it much commended in the accounts given of this poet by French writers of the present day, I have obtained a transcript of it from a public library in this country. If we compared it with Spenser's song in the Shepherd's Calendar, April, we shall find some slight resemblance in the measure, which would induce one to imagine that Colin, though he calls it a lay,

> Which once he made as by a spring he lay,
> And tuned it unto the water's fall,

had yet some snatches of this melody floating in his ear, which mingled themselves with the wilder music.

April, sweet month, the daintiest of all,
    Fair thee befal :
  April, fond hope of fruits that lie
  In buds of swathing cotton wrapt,
    There closely lapt,
  Nursing their tender infancy.

April, that dost thy yellow, green and blue,
    All round thee strew,
  When, as thou go'st, the grassy floor
  Is with a million flowers depeint,
    Whose colours quaint
  Have diaper'd the meadows o'er.

April, at whose glad coming zephyrs rise
    With whisper'd sighs,
  When on their light wing brush away,
  And hang amid the woodlands fresh
    Their aery mesh
  To tangle Flora on her way.

April, it is thy hand that doth unlock,
    From plain and rock,
  Odours and hues, a balmy store,
  That breathing lie on Nature's breast,
    So richly blest
  That earth or heaven can ask no more.

April, thy blooms, amid the tresses laid
    Of my sweet maid,
  Adown her neck and bosom blow ;

And, in a wild profusion there,
    Her shining hair
With them hath blent a golden glow.

April, the dimpled smiles, the playful grace,
    That in the face
Of Cytherea haunt are thine ;
And thine the breath, that from their skies
    The deities
Inhale, an offering at thy shrine.

'Tis thou that dost with summons blithe and soft,
    High up and aloft,
From banishment these heralds bring,
These swallows that along the air
    Scud swift, and bear
Glad tidings of the merry spring,

April, the hawthorn and the eglantine,
    Purple woodbine,
Streak'd pink, and lily-cup, and rose,
And thyme, and marjoram, are spreading,
    Where thou art treading,
And their sweet eyes for thee unclose.

The little nightingale sits singing ay
    On leafy spray,
And in her fitful strain doth run
A thousand and a thousand changes,
    With voice that ranges
Through every sweet division.

April, it is when thou dost come again
      That love is fain
  With gentlest breath the fires to wake
  That cover'd up and slumbering lay,
      Through many a day,
  When winter's chill our veins did slake.

Sweet month, thou see'st at this jocund prime
      Of the spring-time
  The hives pour out their lusty young,
  And hear'st the yellow bees that ply,
      With laden thigh,
  Murmuring the flowery wilds among.

May shall with pomp his wavy wealth unfold,
      His fruits of gold,
  His fertilizing dews, that swell
  In manna on each spike and stem,
      And, like a gem,
  Red honey in the waxen cell.

Who will may praise him ; but my voice shall be,
      Sweet month, for thee ;
  Thou that to her dost owe thy name,
  Who saw the sea-wave's foamy tide
      Swell and divide,
  Whence forth to life and light she came.

Remy Belleau was born at Nogent-le-Rotrou, in le Perche, 1528. René de Lorraine, Marquis of Elbeuf, and General of the French Galleys, committed to him the education of his son. He died in Paris, 1577. Someone said of him, in allusion to the first of his poems above mentioned, that he resolved to construct himself a monument of precious stones.

Besides the editions of his works which I have referred to, there is said to be one printed at Rouen, 1604. 2 vols. 8vo.

JAN ANTOINE DE BAÏF

1532—1592

———

BOTH those of whom I have last spoken, Bellay and Belleau, belonged to that cluster of poets to which was given the name of the French Pleiad. Jodelle, Thyard, Dorat, and Ronsard, were four others in this constellation; and Jan Antoine de Baïf made the seventh, whose lustre, if it were proportioned to the number of verses he has left, would outshine most of them. But, as it is rather by the virtue than the bulk of such luminaries that we appreciate their excellence, he must be satisfied with an inferior place. The chief thing that can be said of him, I think, is that there is much ease in his manner. But this is not enough to carry us through so many books as I have to record the titles of under his name. It is said that no one has had the courage to read them all since his death.

Les Amours de Jan Antoine de Baïf. Paris. Pour Lucas Breyer, 1572. 2 vols. 8vo.

There is what appears to be the same edition with his Passetems added.

In the prefatory address to the Duke of Anjou, afterwards Henry III, he speaks of the French poets who have sung of love. They are Bellay, Thyard, Ronsard, Belleau, to whom he says : " Gentle Belleau, who dost diligently copy nature with exquisite painting, thou hast consecrated the greater part of thy verses to the darling child of Venus." To these he adds Desportes.

Of the four books of his Francine (the name of his mistress), and of his three other books, Des Diverses Amours, there is very little by which I could hope to please my readers. They will, I doubt not, think the following sonnet enough.

On a day, as the winter, relaxing his spleen,
  Grew warm and gave way to the frolicksome spring,
  When all laughs in the fields, and the gay meadows fling
A shower of sweet buds o'er their mantle green,
Twas then in a cave by the wild crankling Clain
  I lay, and sleep shadow'd me o'er with his wing,
  When a lustre shone round, as some angel did bring
A torch that its light from the sunbeams had ta'en ;
And lo ! floating downwards, escorted by Love,
  Nine maids, who methought from one birth might have sprung ;
  And they circled around me and hover'd above,
When one held forth a wreath of green myrtle inwove ;
  See, she cried, that of love some new ditty be sung ;
  And with us thou shalt dwell in our heavenly grove.

He has formed some of these pieces on the model of the Italian canzone, with an envoi at the end.

Besides these are nine books which he calls simply his poems. In the concluding address to his book he has given a portrait of himself.

Another of his publications is, Les Jeux de Jan Antoine de Baïf. Paris. Pour Lucas Breyer. 1573. 8vo. It contains nineteen Eclogues ; Antigone, translated from Sophocles ; two comedies, le Brave and l'Eunuque, the latter from Terence ; and Neuf Devis de Dieux pris de Lucian, nine Dialogues of the Gods, from Lucian. The Eclogues are, for the most part, taken from Theocritus or Virgil. They seem to me among the most pleasing of his poems ; but are sometimes less decorous than one could wish.

" Etre'nes de Poe'zie Fransoeze an vers mezure's, etc., etc., par Jan Antoine de Baïf. Denys du Val. 1574. 8vo. This is a whimsical attempt to imitate the heroic and lyrical measures of the ancients and at the same time to introduce a new mode of orthography, accommodated to the real pronunciation. The book contains, besides a few odes, translations of the works and days of Hesiod, the golden verses of Pythagoras, the admonitory poem that goes under the name of Phocylides, and the Nuptial Advice of Naumachius.

Of what he calls iambikes trimetres nōkadāses, the following compliment to Belleau may be taken as a sample :

> A toe, ki ʒvrier peins le vre, jantil Bélea,
> Nature çerçant kontrefer ân son naïf,
> Ki restes des miens kompanon plus ansïen.

" To thee, gentle Belleau, artist that dost paint the truth, seeking to counterfeit nature to the life, who remainest the oldest associate among my friends, etc."

Some years before, Claudio Tolommei had endeavoured

to naturalize the ancient metres in the Italian tongue, but with no better success.

Jan Antoine de Baïf, the natural son of Lazare de Baïf, Abbot of Genetière, was born in 1532, at Venice, where his father was ambassador. He was much addicted to music; and his concerts were attended by the kings Charles IX and Henry III. I learned from a passage in Burney's History of Music (vol. iii, p. 263), referred to by Mr. Walker in his memoir on Italian Tragedy, Appendix, p. xix, that Baïf usually set his own verses to music. The friendship which Ronsard entertained, for both him and Belleau, will appear in the account that will be given of that poet. He died in 1592. Cardinal du Perron said of him that he was a very good man and a very bad poet. We shall have occasion to estimate the Cardinal's own pretensions in this way.

JAN DE LA PERUSE

d. 1555

—

THE works of Jan de la Peruse, one of those contemporary writers whom we shall see distinguished by Ronsard, were edited by Claude Binet, the affectionate friend of both. He has prefixed a preface to them, and added some verses of his own. The title of this book is, " Les Œuvres de Jan de la Peruse, avec quelques autres diverses Poeses de Claude Binet." A. Lyon. Par Benoist Rigaud, 1577. 16mo. The first poem is Medée, a tragedy. It is a mixture of twelve-syllable verses ; the common verse, ten ; and lyrical, by the chorus. The opening is from Seneca ; but he has not servilely followed either that writer or Euripides. His odes, in the Pindaric style, are much worse than Ronsard's. The most striking thing I have observed in the collection is an ode that was written in his last illness, and which death prevented him from finishing.

> Unto whatever part I turn,
>   Sorrow with me abides ;
> And, creeping o'er my spirit, still,
>   A secret terror glides.

A deadly sound is in mine ears,
  If in the field I be ;
The selfsame sound pursueth still
  When to the woods I flee.

Whatever house I enter in,
  Mirth will no longer stay ;
A sad presage, whereso I come,
  Makes all men haste away.

And, if the people's haunts I shun,
  Seeking a lonely place,
The owl shrieks out in witness to
  My lamentable case.

If to the river-side I go,
  And stand upon the brink,
Sudden the waters, fleeing me,
  Within their channel shrink.

The bird upon the dry thorn sits,
  And not a word saith he :
The very pathway that I tread
  Dries up when touch'd by me.

If any friend perchance do come,
  In pity of my plight,
To comfort me ; he straightway feels
  Himself a wretched wight.

A carking care, a woe extreme,
  Upon his heart do feed ;
And he himself thenceforth, poor man,
  Of comfort much hath need.

This is natural and pathetic. Jan de la Peruse, from the few poems he has left, seems to have been an amiable man, warmly attached to his friends, and not solicitous to court the notice of the powerful. I have learnt nothing more concerning him than that he was born at Angoulême, and died there in 1555, in the prime of his life.

PIERRE DE RONSARD

1524—1585

———

THERE is no poet I am acquainted with, ancient or modern, who has impressed his own character so minutely and strongly on his writings as Ronsard. His loyalty to his sovereigns, accompanied by the most perfect frankness; the openness of his heart, equally disposed to form friend-ships, and constant in preserving them; his generosity and placability; his great learning, that unhappily served, for the most part, only to make him ridiculous; the high value he set on his noble birth,* which, as he said, enabled him to imitate Pindar, when Horace had failed in the attempt on account of his wanting that advantage; his gallantry, made up of pedantry and passion; his hearty love of the country in its natural and unembellished state; his zeal for the poetic art, to which everything else was subordinate—all these, like so many quarterings in a coat of armour, are on his pages blazoned at full, and in their proper colours. From the account which his affectionate friend, Claude Binet, has given of his life, corrected by such notices as he has left of himself, I have extracted some of the principal incidents, and shall place them here as the best

———

* Odes, B. 1, O. xi, Epode iv.

introduction to the remarks which I have to make on his writings.

Pierre de Ronsard, descended from a noble family, was born on Saturday, the eleventh of September, 1524, the year in which Francis I was made prisoner in the battle of Pavia.* The first of his ancestors who came into France was the younger son of an opulent and powerful nobleman settled on the banks of the Danube. This man, incited by a spirit of enterprise, left his home with a band of companions, who, like himself, were younger brothers; and entering into the service of Philip of Valois, then at war with the English, satisfied the French king so well that he was rewarded with an ample estate on the banks of the Loire, where he and his posterity continued to reside. The father of our poet was thought a fit person to accompany Henry, the son of Francis I, when he was sent as a hostage for his father into Spain; and to be entrusted with the management of the young prince's household. Pierre, who was the sixth son, having been brought up till he was nine years old at the Chateau de la Poissoniere, his native place, in the lower Vendomois, was then sent to the Royal College of Navarre at Paris; but, not bearing the restraint laid on him by his preceptors, he was brought by his father to Avignon, and placed in the service of Francis, eldest son of the French king. That prince dying soon after, Ronsard was transferred to the train of his brother Charles, Duke of Orleans, by whom he was again passed over to the retinue of James V, King of Scotland, who had come to marry Madelaine, daughter of the French king. By James he was taken to Scotland, where he

* See his twentieth Elegy, addressed to Remy Belleau.

passed two years and a half. He then spent six months in England, where he learnt our language; and afterwards returned to his former master, the Duke of Orleans, who now retained him as his page. Being master of the accomplishments usual at his age, he was despatched on some affairs to Flanders and Zealand, whence he was charged to proceed on a mission to Scotland. On his second visit to that country he narrowly escaped shipwreck. He returned at the early age of sixteen. Henry, who was afterwards king, then placed him in the suite of Lazare de Baïf, who at that time was ambassador to the Diet at Spires. On this journey he acquired the German language. His next service to his country led him to Piedmont, with the Capitaine de Langey. But these exertions were disproportioned to his time of life, and occasioned a fever, with a defluxion on the brain, that in the end deprived him of his hearing. This misfortune, however, served only to determine him to the pursuit of those studies to which he had not hitherto had time to apply himself. His love of letters is said to have been awakened by one of his brother pages, who had always a Virgil in his hand, and who used to explain to him passages in that poet. In the Preface to the Franciade, he says that his master at school had taught him Virgil, and that, having learnt him by heart from his infancy, he could not forget him. To the Latin poet he now added Jean le Maire de Belges, the Romant de la Rose, and the works of Clement Marot. By Dorat, who was the preceptor of young Baïf, Ronsard was encouraged to the study of Greek, in which he made such a proficiency as to translate the Prometheus of Æschylus; at the same time asking his master why he had so long kept such treasures concealed from him. His next attempt was a version of the Plutus of Aristophanes, part of which still remains. It was represented on the French theatre ; and, from such a beginning, we can, in some measure, account for the excellence at which the French have since arrived in this species of composition. He was next desirous of trying his strength with Pindar, whose manner he was so studious of imitating that he drew on himself the sarcasms of his contemporaries. So far did he carry his admiration of everything that had the most remote connection with his favourite poets of Greece that he is said to have been influenced in the choice of a mistress to celebrate in his verses by the accidental circumstance of her bearing the name of Cassandra, the daughter of Priam. But, in the Epistle to Remy Belleau, he leaves it doubtful whether this was the real or fictitious name of a young lady of whom he became enamoured when he was following the court at Blois.

His idolatry for the antients was not such as to make him neglect the means which his own country afforded him for enriching its vernacular tongue. He is said, like Burke, to have visited the shops of artisans, and to have made himself acquainted with all sorts of handicrafts, in order that he might learn the different terms which were employed in them, and derive illustrations whereby to diversify and ornament his diction. In his Abregé de l'Art Poetique, and in the Preface to the Franciade, he himself recommends this practice, and at the same time advises the poet to appropriate the most significant words that he can collect from the different dialects of France.

About 1549, on his return from Poitiers to Paris, he chanced to fall in with Joachim du Bellay; and, joining together on the journey, the fellow-travellers were so much pleased with one another that they determined to reside under the same roof. In this party Jan Antoine de Baïf made a third. It did not, however, continue uninterrupted by jealousy. Ronsard accused Bellay of wishing to forestall the favour of the public by a collection of poems which he had closely copied from some of his own. He even instituted a suit, as Binet relates, for the recovery of some papers of which du Bellay had surreptitiously obtained possession for this purpose, and gained his cause. But so little resentment was harboured on either side that they renewed the intimacy; and Ronsard encouraged his rival to the cultivation of the art to which he was himself so much attached by means at once more honourable and more likely to ensure success—namely, by trusting to the resources of his own mind. Another instance of his noble temper showed itself in his forgiveness of Mellin de Saint Gelais, who, after having disparaged the works of Ronsard, as he had reason to believe, in the presence of the King, afterwards sought his friendship; whereupon the injured poet not only altered a passage in one of his poems, in which he had expressed his sense of malignity, but honoured him with those praises to which he thought the merit of Saint Gelais entitled him.* In answer to the charges brought against him of obscurity and un-connectedness, he haughtily declared his indifference to

* In the Odes, L. iv, O. xx, it appears that Mellin had disavowed the calumnies which it was reported that he had uttered in the presence of the King against Ronsard; and that their friendship was restored.

the taste of the vulgar; and compared his enemies at the court to dogs that bite at the stone which they cannot digest.

> Mais que ferai-je à ce vulgaire,
> A que jamais je n'ay sceu plaire,
> Ny ne plais, ny plaire ne veux ?
>
> (L. v, O. ii.)

At the end of ten years he quitted his Cassandra, thinking, perhaps, that having stood as long a siege as Troy without yielding, there was no further chance of winning her affections. A young damsel of Anjou, named Mary, was the next object of his poetical courtship. To her he altered his style, and condescended to speak his passion in plainer terms.

Margaret, Duchess of Savoy, is said to have changed the opinion of the French King with respect to the merit of Ronsard, and to have done it so effectually that the monarch afterwards thought himself honoured by possessing so great a genius in his dominions; and gave proofs that he did so by the honours and pensions which he conferred on him, though not in such measure as to satisfy the expectations of Ronsard. The sage, Michel de l'Hôpital, Chancellor to this lady, as he afterwards was of France, also undertook his defence; and wrote a Latin poem in his praise. In return, Ronsard addressed a long and laboured ode (the tenth of the first book) to l'Hôpital. The Cardinal de Chatillon, Charles Cardinal of Lorraine, and other great men of the day, now enlisted themselves in the number of his patrons and friends; and the Presidents of the Jeux Floraux, not thinking the customary prize of the eglantine sufficient for his deserts, sent him a figure of Minerva in silver, which he presented to the King.

At the death of Henry II and during the religious dissensions which followed at the succession of Francis II, Ronsard, in his defence of the established form of worship, exposed himself to some rough treatment from the Reformers. Amongst other things, they accused him of heathenism, for having assisted at the sacrifice of a he-goat; an affair that turned out to be a frolic, in which he and some of his literary companions engaged in consequence of a tragedy by Jodelle being represented before the King. However he might think himself bound to support the ancient religion of his country, that he was no bigot I am disposed to believe from the following lines in an Ode to one of his friends :

> Break not thy peace, nor care a jot
> For Papist or for Huguenot,
> Nor counting either friends or foes,
> Thy trust in God alone repose,
> Who, not like us with partial care,
> Bids all a Father's blessing share.

When the short reign of Francis II was terminated by the death of that king, his brother, Charles IX, did not suffer Ronsard to quit him, by which the poet was much gratified. Amongst other subjects to which Charles directed his pen were such vices in his people as he should think deserving of his satire, at the same time desiring him not to spare what he found worthy of reprehension in himself. Ronsard was hardy enough to take him at his word, and so fortunate as to escape the fate which befell the monitor of the Archbishop of Grenada. The King in his turn kept the bard in good order, declaring that poets were to be used like good steeds, to have sufficient food allowed them, but not to be pampered. The courtiers availed themselves of the fertility of his Muse, and borrowed his pen for the celebration of their mistresses. The Queen Mother, Catherine de Medici, directed him to make choice of one of the ladies of the chamber, whose name was Helene de Surgeres, descended of a Spanish family, to receive the homage of his own person, and bade him address her in the pure and refined style of Petrarch, as most suitable to his age and gravity. Between the discipline thus imposed on him by his royal master and mistress, it is likely that the poet must have felt himself under some constraint. He continued, however, to warble many a sonnet in his cage; and as a reward of his submission and docility was presented with the Abbey of Bellozane and some priories. At the succession of Henry III, to whom he used the same freedom as he had done to his predecessor, he complained that he was no longer caressed as he had been by Charles. He found some consolation in the attentions of the two rival queens, Elizabeth of England and Mary Stewart—the former of whom compared him to a valuable diamond of which she made him a present—and the latter, from her prison, sent him, in 1583, two years before his death, a casket containing two thousand crowns, together with a vase representing Parnassus and Pegasus, and inscribed:

A Ronsard l'Apollon de la Source des Muses.

" To Ronsard, Apollo of the Muses' Fountain."

During the latter part of his life he was much afflicted with the gout. The Sieur Galland, chief of the Academy of Boncourt, was the friend in whose society he now found most comfort, calling him his " second soul." To him, on the twenty-second of October before his death, he wrote : " Qu'il etoit devenu fort foible et maigre depuis quinze jours, qu'il craignit que les feuilles d'Automne ne le vissent tomber avec elles ; que la volonté de Dieu soit faite, et qu'aussi bien parmi tant de douleurs nerveux, ne se pouvant soutenir, il n'etoit plus qu'un inutile fardeau sur la terre, le priant au reste de l'aller trouver, estimant sa presence lui etre un remede." " That for the last fortnight he had become very emaciated and feeble ; that he feared the leaves of Autumn would see him fall with them ; that his prayer, however, was God's will be done ; and that, moreover, not being able to support himself amid such nervous pangs as he endured, he was no longer anything but a useless burthen to the earth ; for the rest, that he entreated him to come and see him, for that he thought his presence would be a cordial to him." Hoping for some ease from change of place and objects, he removed from one of his benefices to another. His piety was fervent and unremitting ; and his repentance for the excesses of his earlier life, into which the court had led him, earnest and sincere. He manifested no uneasiness, except in a frequent desire, which accompanied him to the last, of dictating the verses that presented themselves to his mind. The last were two sonnets, in which he exhorted his spirit to confidence in his Saviour ; and thus he expired on the twenty-seventh of December, 1585, with his hands joined in prayer.

According to his own directions, he was buried in the choir of the church of Saint Cosme en l'Isle, one of his priories, where he died. Claude Binet caused, as he says, a little monument to be erected.

His biographer observes that Europe lost several of her most illustrious men about the same time : one of them was Antoine de Muret, whom Ronsard had reckoned among his friends, and who united with Remy Belleau in writing annotations of his poems.

The French poets, whom he esteemed as having begun to write well in that language, were Maurice Sceve, Hugues Salel, Antoine Heroet, Mellin de Saint Gelais, Jacques Pelletier, and Guillaume Autels. To them succeeded a set of writers who were in some measure, though older some of them than himself, influenced by his example, and who have been already mentioned as constituting, together with him, the French Pleiad.   Others, whom he highly esteemed were Estienne Pasquier ;   Olivier de Magny ;   Jean de la Peruse ; Amadis Jamyn, whom he had educated as his page ; Robert Garnier, a tragic writer ;   Florent Chrestien ; Scevole de Sainte Marthe ;   Jean Passerat ;   Philippe Desportes ; the Cardinal du Parron ; and Bertaud. Among those learned foreigners who paid their tribute to the excellence of Ronsard occur the distinguished names of Julius Cæsar Scaliger, Pietro Vettori, and Sperone Speroni.

His conversation is said to have been easy and pleasant. He was himself free, open and simple ; and associated willingly with none who were otherwise, being a declared enemy to everything like affectation.   In short, Claude Binet considered him in manners and appearance as the model of a true French gentleman.

His usual residence was at Sainte Cosme, a delightful spot (l'œillet de la Touraine), the pink of Touraine, itself the garden of France ; or at Bourgueil, where he went for the sake of sporting, in which he took great pleasure ; and here he kept the dogs given him by Charles IX, a falcon, a goshawk (un teircelet d'autour). Another of his amusements was gardening, in which he had considerable skill. When at Paris, his favourite retirements were at Meudon, for the sake of the woods and the Seine ; or at Gentilly, Hercueil, Saint Cloud, and Vanves, for the sake of the rivulet of Biévre and its fountains. He took delight also in the sister arts of painting, sculpture and music, and was skilled enough in the latter to sing his own verses.

The poems that stand first in his collection are the Amours de Cassendre, consisting, besides a few other pieces, of two hundred and twenty-two sonnets, one only of which is in the Alexandrine, the rest are in the vers communs, or deca-syllabick measure. In the Preface to the Franciade he says that he had changed his mind as to the Alexandrine measure, which he no longer considered as the proper heroic. His reason is, that it savours too much of an extremely easy prose, and is too enervated and flagging ; except it be for translations, in which it is useful on account of its length, for expressing the sense of an author. He thought differently when he wrote his Art Poetique, as may be seen by referring to the chapter on versification.

Ronsard must sometimes have puzzled Cassandra, unless she was tolerably learned and well read in Aristotle. Thus in Sonnet 68 he asks her :

> O Lumiere ! enrichie
> D'un feu divin, qui m'ard si vivement,
> Pour me donner l'etre et le mouvement,
> Etes vous pas me seul entelechie ?

> " O light ! in whom I see
> The fire divine, that burns me to bestow
> Whate'er of being or of life I know,
> Say, art not thou my sole entelechy ? "

In the 104th he reminds her of the violation of her person by Ajax, the son of Oileus.

His attempt to mould the French language to the purposes of poetry did not succeed. When, in imitation of Petrarch, he says—

> Le seul Avril, de son jeune printemps
> Endore, emperle, enfrange notre temps.
>> (Son. 121.)
> Vedi quant' arte 'ndora e'mperla e'nnostra
> L'abito eletto—

the French being the language of Europe will not easily endure such innovations as these, which tend to make it less generally intelligible.

The fifty-second sonnet is no unfavourable specimen of his Platonic manner :

> Or ever Love drew forth the slumbering light,
>> That in the bosom of old Chaos lay,
>> Earth, sea, and sky, without its primal ray,
>> Were in blank ruin sunk and formless night :

So, whelm'd in sloth, erewhile, my heavy spright
   Did in a dull and senseless body stray,
   Scarce life enough to stir the lumpish clay,
   Till from thine eyes Love's arrow pierc'd my sight
Then was I quicken'd; and, by Love inform'd,
   My being to a new perfection came :
   His influence my blood and spirits warm'd;
And, as I mounted this low world above,
   Following in thought and soul his sacred flame,
   Love was my being, and my essence Love.

The fifty-ninth is an imitation of Bembo. There is
more elasticity and freedom in the copy than in the
original.

As when fresh spring apparels wood and plain,
   Forth from his native lair, a tender fawn
   Issues alone and careless, if the dawn
   'Gin the grey east with flecker'd crimson stain ;
And all unheeding of the hunter's train,
   Wherever through his roving fancy drawn,
   By lake or river, hill or flowery lawn,
   Sports with light foot, and feeds and sports
      again ;
Nor aught he fears from meshes or from bow,
   Till to his liver a fleet arrow sped
   Has pierced, and panting on the earth he lies :
In my life's April thus wont I go,
   Of harm unfearing, where my fancy led,
   Ere the dart reached me from her radiant eyes.

The hundred and sixty-second, to Baïf, proves his

high esteem for that writer, whom we have seen so much disparaged.

The conclusion of this is from Petrarch :

> Ma pur si espre vie e si selvagge
>> Cercar non sò, ch'Amor non venga sempre
>> Ragionando con meco, ed io con lui,

where the variety in the metre gives the Italian poet a striking advantage over Ronsard.

> Baïf, who, second in our age to none,
>> Dost with free step to Virtue's summit mount,
>> While thou allay'st thine ardour at the fount
>> Of Ascra, where the Muses met their son ;
> An exile I, where sloping to the sun
>> Rich Sabut lifts his grape-empurpled mount,
>> Am fain to waste mine hours, and pensive count
>> Loire's wond'ring waves as oceanward they run.
> And oft, to shun my cares, the haunt I change,
>> Now linger in some nook the stream beside,
>> Now seek a wild wood, now a cavern dim.
> But all avails not : whereso'er I range,
>> Love still attends, and ever at my side
>> Conversing with me walks, and I with him.

There is more nature and passion in the two hundred and fourteenth sonnet, which begins :

> Quand je te voy, discourant à par toy,

than I have observed in any of the others.

The Second Book of his Amours, which contains,

besides other short poems, eighty sonnets, is devoted
to the praises of his Marie, the last thirteen being written
after her death. It is confessedly in a more familiar
style than the First Book; yet is filled with images
drawn from the heathen mythology.

Two flowers I love, the March-flower and the rose,
  The lovely rose that is to Venus dear,
  The March-flower that her the name doth bear,
  Who will not leave my spirit in repose :
Three birds I love ; one, moist with May-dew, goes
  To dry his feathers in the sunshine clear ;
  One for his mate laments throughout the year,
  And for his child the other wails his woes :
And Bourgueil's pine I love, where Venus hung,
  For a proud trophy on the darksome bough,
  Ne'er since releas'd, my youthful liberty :
And Phœbus' tree love I, the laurel tree,
  Of whose fair leaves, my mistress, when I sung,
  Bound with her locks a garland for my brow.

In one of his odes (Book V, O. xi) he again expresses
his preference for these two flowers, the rose and the
violet, which he calls the flower of March and supposes
to bear the name of his Marie. That the lark was his
favourite bird appears from a passage in his Gayetez :

                  Alouette,
        Ma doucelette mignolette,
        Qui plus qu'un rossignol me plais
        Qui chante en un bocage epais.

After a few sonnets and madrigals on another lady,

whom he calls Astrée, and of whom we are not told whether she was of the Queen Mother's choosing or his own, we proceed to his two books of sonnets on Helene. These are a hundred and forty-two in number. He begins with swearing to her by her brothers Castor and Pollux; by the vine that enlaced the elm; by the meadows and woods, then sprouting into verdure (it was the first day of May); by the young Spring, eldest son of Nature; by the crystal that rolled along the streams; and by the nightingale, the miracle of birds—that she should be his last venture.

> Ce premier jour de May, Hélène, je vous jure
> Par Castor, par Pollux, vos deux freres jumeaux,
> Par la vigne enlassée à l'entour des ormeaux,
> Par les prez, par les bois herissez de verdure,
> Par le nouveau printemps fils aisné de nature,
> Par le crystal qui roule au giron des ruisseaux,
> Et par le rossignol, miracle des oiseaux,
> Que seule vous serez ma dernier avanture.
>
> (Son. 1.)

Whether she was so or not, does not, I think, appear; but it is full time, for he was about fifty years old. There is, however, another short book, entitled Amours Diverses; and, besides this, a large gleaning of sonnets and odes, many of them on the same subject, which he did not think worth gathering; but which his editors were careful enough to pick up and store along with the rest. Amongst these are some which for more reasons than one I cannot recommend to the notice of my reader. We will pass them, and go on to his odes.

These may be divided into two classes ; some, in which he has imitated the ancients ; and others, that are the offspring of his own feelings and fancy. In the former, unhappily the larger number, Anacreon, Pindar, Callimachus, Horace, are all laid under contribution by turns, and that with no sparing hand. It was in his ability to transfuse the spirit of the old Theban into Gallic song, or, as he called it, to Pindarise, that he most prided himself, and it was here that he most egregiously failed.

> Si dès mon enface
> Le premier en France
> J'ai Pindarisé,
> De telle entreprise
> Heureusement prise
> Je ne voy prisé.

Nothing can well be more unlike the poet, whom he boasts to have introduced into his own language, than this tripping measure. As for the music of Pindar, indeed, that was out of the question. It was not in the power of the French, nor perhaps of any other language, to return even a faint echo of it. But those who are acquainted with that poet know that another of his distinctions consists, not only in the hardiness of his metaphors, but in the no less light than firm touch with which he handles them. One instance will be enough to show how ill Ronsard has represented this characteristic of his model. Pindar, speaking of a man who had not, through neglect or forgetfulness, his task to do when it ought to have been already done, says that " he did not come, bringing with him Excuse, the daughter of

Afterthought " ; or, literally, " of the late-minded Epimetheus."

How has Ronsard contrived to spoil this in his application of it to the Constable Montmorency!

> Qui seul mettoit en evidence
> Les saints tressors de sa prudence,
> Ne s'est jamais accompagné
> Du sot enfant d'Epimethee,
> Mais de celuy de Promethée,
> Par longues ruses enseigné.
>
> (L. I, O. i, Strophe 6.)

Another of Pindar's excellences are those γνῶμαι, sentences, or maxims, the effect of which results not more from their appositeness than their compression. One of these is that " Envy is better than pity," which Ronsard has left indeed no longer one of the dark sayings of the wise, but has made almost ludicrous by the light in which he has placed it :

> C'est grand mal d'etre miserable,
> Mais c'est grand bien d'etre envié.
>
> (L. I, O. x, Strophe 22.)

Sometimes on Pindar's stock he engrafts a conceit, than which no fruit can be more alien to the parent tree. Thus, of a passage in the Second Pythian, vv. 125 to 130, in which the Theban appears to intimate, as he does elsewhere more plainly, that he expects a reward for his song, Ronsard avails himself to tell his patron that he shall see how liberally his praises will sound if " a present gilds the chord " :

Prince, je t'envoye cette ode,
Trafiquant mes vers à la mode
Que le marchand baille son bien,
Troque pour troq' : toy qui es riche,
Toy Roy des biens, ne soit point chiche
De changer ton present au mien.
Ne te lasse point de donner,
Et tu verras comme j'accorde
L'honneur que je promets sonner,
Quand un present dore ma corde.

(L. I, O. i, Antis. 8.)

This is truly anti-Pindaric.

Of that other class of odes, which appear more like the overflowing of his own mind, and which have a better chance of pleasing the English reader at least, I would point out the following : in the first book, the seventeenth ; in the second, the eleventh, to his preceptor Jean Dorat, and the eighteenth to his lacquey ; in the third, the eighth to the fountain Bellerie, the twenty-first to Gaspar D'Auvergne, and the two following it ; in the fourth book, ode the fourth, on the choice of his burial-place, together with the eighteenth and nineteenth ; and, in the fifth and last book, odes eleven and seventeen.

God shield ye, heralds of the spring,
Ye faithful swallows fleet of wing,
    Houps, cuckoos, nightingales,
Turtles, and every wilder bird,
That make your hundred chirpings heard
    Through the green woods and dales.

God shield ye, Easter daisies all,
Fair roses, buds and blossoms small;
   And ye, whom erst the gore
Of Ajax and Narciss did print,
Ye wild thyme, anise, balm, and mint,
   I welcome ye once more.

God shield ye, bright embroider'd train
Of butterflies, that, on the plain,
   Of each sweet herblet sip;
And ye new swarm of bees that go
   Where the pink flowers and yellow grow
   To kiss them with your lip.

A hundred thousand times I call—
   A hearty welcome on ye all:
   This season how I love!
This merry din on every shore,
For winds and storms, whose sullen roar
   Forbade my steps to rove.

———

   Fair hawthorn flowering,
   With green shade bowering
Along this lovely shore;
   To thy foot around
   With his long arms wound
A wild vine has mantled thee o'er.

In armies twain,
    Red ants have ta'en
Their fortress beneath thy stock :
    And, in clefts of thy trunk,
    Tiny bees have sunk
A cell where their honey they lock.

    In merry spring-tide,
    When to woo his bride
The nightingale comes again,
    Thy boughs among,
    He warbles the song
That lightens a lover's pain.

    'Mid thy topmost leaves,
    His nest he weaves
Of moss and the satin fine,
    Where his callow brood
    Shall chirp at their food,
Secure from each hand but mine.

    Gentle hawthorn, thrive,
    And for ever live,
Mayst thou blossom as now in thy prime ;
    By the wind unbroke,
    And the thunder-stroke,
Unspoil'd by the axe or time.

In several of his odes there are passages of extraordinary splendour. What can exceed in magnificence this description of Jupiter coming in the form of a swan to Leda ?

His plumes beneath are glittering bright
    With such a golden glow
As when the broad eye of the night
    Is on the earliest snow.
He shaketh once his outspread wing,
    And cleaves the sky amain,
And at one stroke his new oars fling
    The billowy air in twain.

One of his odes concludes with a wish, to the completion of which I would willingly contribute. After invoking the other heathen deities, he adds :

Ye dryads and ye fays that bind
Your brows with simple reed entwined ;
Who down the crystal rivers swim,
Turning the bends with lithesome limb ;
And ye, that in the green bark dwell,
Meek sisters of the quiet dell ;

With ivy deck this favour'd page ;
And let my lyre from age to age
Still echo on, in strains that rise
Above this mean earth to the skies,
Till, at the world's extremest bounds,
The Moor and Briton learn the sounds.

The seventeenth ode of the same book is prettily rendered from the well-known idyllium, whether it be Moschus's or Bion's. Ronsard's version of it much excels that by Claudio Tolommei, inserted by Mr. Mathias in his selections from the Lyrical Poets of Italy, V. iii.

p. 227. There have been several attempts to imitate
it in our own language. I will not now add another to
the number.

The third ode of the fifth book is addressed to three
English ladies, who had composed a book of Christian
Distichs in Latin ; which, it is said in a note by
Richelet, had been translated into Greek, Italian and
French, and inscribed to Margaret, sister to Henry II ;
as Michel de L'Hôpital had remarked in his Third
Epistle.

The eleventh and twelfth odes are attempts at the
Sapphic measure. One, and I believe one only, is in
blank verse. It is the eleventh in the third book.

It is wonderful how much learning and pains his
commentators have thrown away on these poems.
Nothing can more prove the high esteem in which they
were then held.

His Franciade succeeds next. The death of his patron,
Charles IX, discouraged him from continuing it, and he
has left only four books, which like most of his other
writings are composed of shreds of the Greek and Latin
poets, but with some splendid patches of his own interspersed among them.

At the end of the fourth book he has very candidly
added this confession :

" The Frenchman who shall read my verses, if
they be not Greeks and Romans, too, instead of this
book will have but a cumbersome weight in their
hands."

The hero, Francus, was the same person with Astyanax,
and is said to have derived his new name from the Greek
compound epithet Pheréenchos, Porte-lance.

All this affectation of antiquity is not very consistent with the anger expressed in his Preface against those who, neglecting their vernacular tongues, composed in the Greek and Latin. " Encore vaudoit-il mieux, comme un bon bourgeois ou citoyen, rechercher et faire un lexicon des viels mots d'Artus, Lancelot, et Gauain, ou commenter le Romant de la Rose, que s'amuser à je ne scai quelle grammaire Latine qui a passé son temps."
—" It would be better, like some good burgess or citizen, to search for and make a lexicon of old words from Arthur, Lancelot, or Gawen, or to write notes on the Romant of the Rose, than to amuse oneself with I know not what Latin grammar, that is now completely out of date."

There is nothing in the Franciade with which I have been so much pleased as with the meeting between Francus and Hyante. It is copied from Apollonius Rhodius and Valerius Flaccus, but surpasses both.

> Ils sont long temps sans deviser ensemble
> Tous deux meuts l'un devant l'autre assis :
> Ainsi qu'on voit, quand l'air est bien rassis,
> Deux pins plantez aux deux bords du rivage,
> Ne remuer ny cime ny fueillage,
> Cois et sans bruit en attendant le vent ;
> Mais quant il souffle et les pousse en avant,
> L'un pres de l'autre en murmurant se jettent
> Cime sur cime, et ensemble caquettent.
> Ainsi devoient babiller à leur tour
> Ces deux Amans.
>
> (L. iv.)

Between Charles IX and Ronsard there passed some pleasant verses. The monarch bantered him on his old age, but concluded by owning his own inferiority in the gifts of mind.

> Par ainsi je conclu, qu'en scavoir tu me passe,
> Dautant que mon printemps tes cheveux gris efface.

The poet replied by reminding him that he must some day be like himself.

> Charles tel que je suis vous serez quelque jour—

that youth is the season of danger and temptation, and that old age has many advantages over it; that the King was wrong to call him old, for that he should yet be able to serve His Majesty at least twenty years longer. He ended by a courteous avowal that if Charles would but take a little pains he might be as good a poet as himself.

To the succeeding monarch, Henry III, he was not sparing of good advice.

> Think not in France thy voyage, King, shall be
> O'er the smooth face of an unruffled sea :
> O'er her swoln waves the blasts of faction sweep,
> And warring zealots lash the angry deep.
> Her heart is stubborn.   But thou must not goad
> Her rage, or think to tame her by the rod.
> Time's lenient hand her senses will restore :
> Chastise the furious, and they storm the more.
> Be these thy cards and compass—to make light
> The people's burdens, and to rule by right ;

For the state's welfare all thy plans to frame,
War thine aversion, peace thy love and aim ;
To chuse for council men most sage and skill'd ;
To pay thy creditors, nor ever build ;
Grave in apparel, faithful to thy word ;
Nor suffer, though a free and courteous lord,
One sycophant or liar at thy board.

He earnestly exhorted Charles IX to deliver the Greeks from the tyranny of their Turkish masters :

Grecia, the world's fair light, that on this earth
Ne'er had, nor e'er will have, her like in worth,
Demands thine arm of Christian Majesty,
To set her neck from this base bondage free.

In his verses to Queen Elizabeth he describes England ; and, having said that Bacchus alone of the gods had denied it his gifts, he passes an encomium on its native liquor, which would lead one to conclude that the bard had enjoyed his cup of mild ale in this country, as much as he did the bottle of wine that was brought to him from the nearest village, under a hawthorn tree, in his own.

When Ceres o'er the world's four parts had stray'd,
Seeking in every clime the ravish'd maid ;
She, while her hands two piny torch-lights bore,
Came faint and weary to thy distant shore.
A beverage then instead of wine she gave
In golden plenty o'er thy fields to wave ;

Not violent or strong ; nor apt to fire
The troubled brain, and deathful deeds inspire.
Named for herself, as the fair harvest grew,
She call'd its smiling produce mild cwrw.*
The neighbours quaff the novel cups with glee,
The social share the harmless jollity.

In his verses to Catherine de Medici, he tells her that
Nature after making her had broken the mould.

Elle en rompit le moule, à fin que sans pareille
Tu fusses ici-bas du monde la merveille.
(Ibid. p. 731.)

The Bocage Royal is followed by the Eclogues. At
the beginning of the first he commends the beauty of
nature unadorned and wild beyond all the embellish-
ments of art.

Car tousiours le nature est meilleure que l'art.

Among the other sovereigns of Europe, he eulogizes
Elizabeth and Mary.

Next pass'd I to the British nation o'er,
A land right opposite to Gallia's shore,
I saw the wild waves of their ocean-flood ;
I saw their chaste Queen, beautiful and good.
Her palace with great lords was throng'd about,
Fair, courteous, wise, magnanimous, and stout.
I saw them cordially to France inclined ;
Our ancient feuds delivered to the wind ;

* The British name for ale, pronounced cooroo.

For they had vow'd, henceforth with heart sincere,
To love her people, and her kings revere.
I saw the Scottish Queen, so fair and wise,
She seem'd some power descended from the skies.
Near to her eyes I drew : two burning spheres
They were, two suns of beauty, without peers.
I saw them dimm'd with dewy moisture clear,
And trembling on their lids a crystal tear ;
Remembering France, her sceptre, and the day
When her first love pass'd like a dream away.
Whoe'er should mark the two Queens in their
pride
Of beauty, traversing the foamy tide,
Would surely say, in wonder lost the while,
Two Venuses approach their favourite isle.

In the third Eclogue we have the chief poets of his
day, under the names of shepherds. Bellot is Bellay ;
and Perrot, Ronsard himself ; Janot is Jean Dorat ;
Micheau, Michel de l'Hôpital ; Lancelot, Lancelot
Carles, a great poet, says the annotator Marcassus ;
and Bellin, Belleau.

In the fourth Eclogue, some of these appear again.
In the fifth we have the two royal brothers, Charles IX
and Henry III, as shepherds, with the names of Carlin
and Xandrin.

In the second of the Elegies, Ronsard warns his friend
Philippe Desportes against harassing his mind with too
much study.

After the Elegies come two books of Hymns. Towards
the end of the third, in the first book, he has made
bad work of the story of the Gemini and Idas, which is

so beautifully told in Pindar. The seventh, entitled
Daimons, is a curious collection of the superstitions
that prevailed in his time respecting spirits. Book II,
hymn ii, he runs a strange parallel between Hercules
and Jesus Christ. Hymn xiii of the Husbandmen to
Saint Blaise is exceedingly pretty.

The first book of Poems which is next in order is
inscribed to Mary Stewart, whose captivity he deplores,
and blames the cruelty of Elizabeth. In the second poem
to her (p. 1174), he represents her leaving Fontainebleau
to return to Scotland. In describing the colour of her
eyes, which he calls " un peu Brunet," he says :

> Aussi le Grecs en amour les premiers
> Ont à Pallas Déese des guerriers
> Donné l'œil verd, et le brun a Cythere.

There is a great deal of heart in these verses to the unhappy Queen of the Scots. Saying that she sometimes
chuses some of his own poems for her reading, he
adds :

> Car je ne veux en ce monde choisir
> Plus grand honneur que vous donner plaisir.

" I would not chuse in this world a greater honour than
to give you pleasure."

And towards the conclusion of this Envoy, as it is
called :

" She is courteous as she is, O glorious book, receiving
thee with joyful face, and, stretching out her hand to
thee kindly, will ask thee how Ronsard is, what he is
doing, what he is saying, what his present state is : thou

shalt say to her that there is nothing here which gives him pleasure, etc."

We cannot leave Ronsard more honourably employed than in thus endeavouring to alleviate the sufferings of an oppressed and perhaps innocent woman.

ESTIENNE JODELLE

1532—1573

—

THE first of the French poets who made a figure in tragedy was Estienne Jodelle. He was the intimate of Ronsard, and had a place in the French Pleiad. His Cleopatre, which was performed in the presence of Henry II and his court, pleased that monarch so well that he immediately made the author a present of five hundred crowns. On this occasion, a he-goat crowned with ivy, his beard and horns gilded, was led in mock procession to Bacchus; and the sacrifice accompanied by a dithyrambic effusion from the muse of Jan Antoine de Baïf : all this to the great scandal of the reformers. At the opening of this play, the ghost of Antony appears, and ushers in the argument in the same manner as the ghost of Polydorus does in the Hecuba of Europides, and that of Ninus in the Semiramis of Manfredi and of Voltaire. Cleopatra then enters with Eras and Charmium, and tells them that she has seen Antony in a dream, and that he calls her to follow him. She declares her resolution to die rather than be led in triumph by Octavius Cæsar. The other dramatis personæ are Octavius, Agrippa, Proculeius, and a chorus of Alexandrian women. Octavius expostulates with her for her conduct towards Octavia, the wife of Antony. Cleopatra endeavours to appease him by discovering to him her treasures. Seleucus, one of her vassals, who is present, declares she has not shown the whole of them, on which the Queen cuffs and drags him by the hair, and he flies to Octavius for protection. The indignation expressed by Cleopatra to Eras and Charmium against Octavius when he is gone out ; her resolution to die, again repeated ; her lamentation over Antony ; and the account given by Proculeius of her death, make up the rest of this tragedy.

I shall extract a short passage descriptive of her sorrow and despair.

Eras

Ah death ! O gentle death ; death, only cure
Of spirits sunk in a strange prison-house ;
Why sufferest thou thy rights thus trampled on ?
Say, have we wrong'd thee, gentle, gentle death ?
Why hastest not thy step, O lingering Fate ?
Why wilt thou bear the durance of this bond,
Which shall not know the boon of freedom till
This spirit be deliver'd by thy dart ?
Speed them, oh, speed thee : thou shalt have to boast
That thou hast e'en from Cæsar won a spoil.

.   .   .   .   .   .

Cleopatra

Let us then die, sweet sisters ; having rather
The courage to serve Pluto than this Cæsar ;

But, ere we die, it doth behove us make
The obsequies of Antony ; and then to die
Becomes us.   I've sent word hereof but now
To Cæsar, who consents that I should honour
My master and—ah me ! my lover thus.
Stoop then, O Heaven, and ere I die come see
This the last mourning I shall ever make.
Perhaps 'twill grieve thee to have dealt thus with me,
Repenting thee of such strange moral sorrow.
Come then, sweet sisters ; wailings, groans and tears
Shall weaken us so much that at the last
Death will no longer scare us when we've made
An opening for our spirits half-way to meet him.

There is in Maffei's collection an Italian tragedy on
the same subject, by the Cardinal Delfino.   It is full of
moral reflections, and the choruses have nothing to do
with the business of the piece.   Yet there is some pathos
in the description of Cleopatra's death.

In the Didon, Jodelle's other tragedy (which is
written in the Alexandrine measure) the speeches are
long, and often tedious ; but there is more of what
we should call poetry in it than in the tragedies
of Corneille and Racine, or than in the Didon of Le
Franc de Pompignan, who is one of the best of that
school.

La Didone and la Cleopatra occur in the catalogue of
tragedies written by Giambattista Giraldi Cinthio, in
whose novels Shakespeare has been so much indebted.
He was contemporary with Jodelle, having been born in
1504, and deceased in 1569.

L'Eugene, a comedy, revolts us by a mixture of low

intrigue, indecency and profaneness.   Of the last, one sample will suffice.

> Avez vous en vostre maison
> Grand nombre de fils ?—Trois—Je prise
> Ce nombre qui est sainct.

In his sonnets, the conceits are strained, and the language rugged.

The following, I believe, is as free from these imperfections as any of the number.

> I love the bay-tree's never withering green,
>   Which nor the northern blast nor hoary rime
>   Effaceth ; conqueror of death and time ;
>   Emblem wherein eternity is seen :
> I love the holly and those prickles keen
>   On his gloss'd leaves that keep their verdant prime ;
>   And ivy, too, I love, whose tendrils climb
>   On tree or bower, and weave their amorous skreen.
> All three I love, which always green resemble
>   Th' immortal thoughts that in my heart assemble
>   Of thee, whom still I worship night and day.
> But straiter far the knot that hath me bound,
>   More keen my thorns, and greener is my wound,
>   Than are the ivy, holly or green bay.

His Ode de la Chasse au Roy contains much that would interest those who are curious about the manner of sporting in that time.

The lively minuteness with which he has delineated the death of the stag would do credit to the pencil of Sir Walter Scott.

Now at his haunch the fleet hound hangs,
   Now on the earth behold him lie :
They tear him with relentless fangs,
   Rejoicing in their victory.
Big drops are falling from his eyes ;
   And, though well nigh we mourn his case,
   Behoveth that of such a chase
His death must be the glorious prize.

The stag's death-note is sounded : then
   From mountain, valley, rock and glen,
Loud peals in thundering echoes sound,
   Which the raised clarions scatter round.
One of his right feet shorn away,
   The antlers from his forehead torn,
   Meet ensigns, Sire, thy pomp adorn ;
Thy trophies in the bloody fray.

From this poem most of the terms used in hunting
and falconry might probably be collected.

All words of venery,
Or what to other sports belong,
   Whether of sight, or quest, or chase,
   Or taking after weary race :
All that may not be told in song
Are there esteem'd a goodly lore.

Jodelle was born in Paris in 1532, and died in a state
of poverty, occasioned, I doubt, by his own indiscretion,
in 1573. The edition of his works, to which the above
references have been made, is entitled, Les Œuvres et

Meslanges Poetiques d'Estienne Jodelle, Sieur du Ly-
modin. A Paris, chez Nicholas Chesneau, rue sainct
Jacques, à l'enseigne du Chesne verd, et Mamert Patisson,
rue sainct Jean de Beavais devant les escholes de Decret.
1574.

PHILIPPE DESPORTES

1546—1606

BOILEAU, in the first canto of his Art
Poetique, has drawn a slight and rapid
sketch of the progress which the French
poetry had made before his own time. To Villon
he attributed the first improvement on the confusion and grossness of the old romancers. Soon after,
Marot succeeded; and under his hands flourished the
ballad, triolet, and mascarade; the rondeau assumed a
more regular form, and a new mode of versifying was
struck out. Ronsard next embroiled everything by his
ill-directed efforts to reduce the art into order. In the
next generation, his Muse, who had spoken Greek and
Latin in French, saw her high-swelling words and her
pedantry fallen into disesteem; and the failure of the
boastful bard rendered Desportes and Bertaut more
cautious.

> Ce poëte orgueilleux trébuché de si haut
> Rendit plus retenus Desportes et Bertaut.

Boileau would have done well to temper the severity
of this censure on Ronsard, who had more genius than
himself. There is, however, some truth in what he has
said of Desportes and Bertaut. They were much less

bold than their predecessor; nor is it unlikely that the excesses into which he had run might have increased their natural timidity; though it will be seen that the latter of these two writers, especially, held him in the utmost veneration. They both in a great measure desisted from the attempt made by those who had gone before them to separate the language of poetry from that of prose, not more by its numbers than by the form and mould of its phrases and words; and, although they were not ambitious of the extreme purity and refinement which Malherbe afterwards affected, and on which his countrymen have since so much prided themselves, yet by their sparing use of the old licences they made the transition less difficult than it would otherwise have been.

Of the works of Desportes, printed at Rouen in 1611, a few years after his death, a large proportion consists of sonnets. They amount all together to about four hundred in number, and turn for the most part on the subject of love. The following bears some resemblance to an exquisite song of Mrs. Barbauld's, beginning:

> Come here, fond youth, whoe'er thou be,
> That boasts to love as well as me.

> If this be love, to bend on earth the sight,
>   To speak in whisper'd sounds, and often sigh,
>   To wander lonely with an inward eye
>   Fix'd on the fire that ceaseth day nor night,
> To paint on clouds in fitting colours bright,
>   To sow on waves, and to the winds to cry,
>   To look for darkness when the light is high,
>   And, when the darkness comes, to look for light:

If this be love, to love oneself no more,
  To loathe one's life, and for one's death implore :
  Then all the loves do in my bosom dwell.
Yet herein merit for myself I claim,
  That neither racks, imprisonment, nor flame,
  Avowal of my passion can compel.

The invitation to a weary traveller, in another of his sonnets, is unusually elegant :

This cool spring, and its waters silver-clean,
  In gentle murmurs seem to tell of love ;
  And all about the grass is soft and green ;
  And the close alders weave their shade above ;
The sidelong branches to each other lean,
  And, as the west wind fans them, scarcely move ;
  The sun is high in midday splendour sheen,
  The heat has parch'd the earth and soil'd the grove.
Stay, traveller, and rest thy limbs awhile,
  Faint with the thirst, and worn with heat and toil ;
  Where thy good fortune brings thee, traveller, stay.
Rest to thy wearied limbs will here be sweet,
  The wind and shade refresh thee from the heat,
  And the cool fountain chase thy thirst away.

The character of ease and sweetness, which he maintains in such verses as these, is often deserted for quaintness and conceit. At times, indeed, he is most extravagant, as in Sonnet LXI, where he tells his mistress that they shall both go to the infernal regions—she for her rigour, and himself for having foolishly followed his desires ; that, provided Minos adjudges them to the same place, all will be well—her sufferings will be exasperated by their being near to each other, and his will be turned into joy by the sight of her charms.

> Car mon ame ravie en l'objet de vos yeux,
> Au milieu des enfers establira les cieux,
> De la gloire eternelle abondamment pourveuë :
> Et quand tous les damnez si voudront émouvoir
> Pour empescher ma gloire, ils n'auront le pouvoir
> Pourveu qu'estant là bas je ne perde la veuë.

In another place (Diane, L. II, S. xlviii, p. 137) he has the same thought of their being both condemned, but draws a different conclusion from it.

In the Chant d'Amour (p. 66) there is a mixture of metaphysics and allegory, such as we sometimes meet in Spenser, and that would not have disgraced that writer.

> Grace, whereso'er thou walkest, still precedes ;
> A lively carol, Pleasure round thee leads ;
> And Care, the harpy, which makes men his prey,
> Flees at thy coming like the wind away.

In his Procez contre Amour au Siege de la Raison (p. 70) he introduces himself pleading at the bar of Reason against Love, who refutes the poet's charges with much eloquence.

> I made him from the city's crowd retire,
> I cleansed his bosom from each low desire,
> Companion of the sylvan deities ;

I chased the fiend Ambition from his side,
With Guile and Envy, Avarice and Pride,
That rack the courts of kings in cruel wise.

.   .   .   .   .   .

I bade him raise his view and prune his wings
For the blest dwelling of immortal things ;
I prisoner held the more to make him free.

The conclusion is equally unexpected and sprightly :

Then both were silent, waiting the decree
Of Reason, who towards us held her view :
Your subject of debate is such, she cried,
It asks a longer session to decide.
That said, she laugh'd, and suddenly withdrew.

There are a few lines on his mistress Hippolyte, which
are a pitch above the usual strain of love verses.

Features of warlike maid,
    Such as life in antique story ;
A heavenly port ; a light display'd ;
    A spirit warm with love of glory ;
High discourses, thoughts divine ;
    A thousand virtues met in one :
    These are the sorceries have won
This prison'd heart of mine.

He expresses a hope that the fame of his mistress will
rival that of Laura.

I trust, in time, her lovely branch will rise,
Rear'd by my numbers, to the starry skies ;
And Florence boast no more that scornful maid
She saw transform'd into a laurel shade.

If Petrarch were in any danger of being eclipsed by Desportes, it would be from the veil which he has cast over his lustre in those passages of which he has attempted a translation into French. The reader will see an instance of this inferiority by comparing the well-known sonnet,

Solo e pensoso i più deserti campi,

with Desportes, S. xlv, p. 201.

A pas lens et tardifs tout seul je me promaine.

He did not wish to conceal the numerous obligations he lay under to the Italian poets ; and, when a book was written with a design of showing how much the French had taken from them, good-humouredly observed that, if he had been apprised of the author's intention to expose him, he could have contributed largely to swell the size of the volume.

If he has made thus free with the property of others, there are those who in their turn have not scrupled to borrow from him. Some stanzas in an admired ode by Chaulieu, on his native place, Fontenai, must have been suggested by the pathetic complaint which Desportes supposes to be uttered by Henry III at Fontainebleau where that monarch first saw the light.

> Nymphs of the forest, in whose arms I lay
> Nurs'd in soft slumbers from my natal day,
>   Now that my weary way is past
> Desert me not ; but as ye favouring smiled,
> And weaved a cradle for me when a child,
>   Oh, weep, and weave my bier at last.

The song at the beginning of the Bergeries and Masquerades is exceedingly sprightly and gracious. I will add another, which, though scarce less animated, is in a graver style.

> Alas ! how hard a lot have we
>   That live the slaves of men's decrees,
>   As full of vain inconstancy
>   As are the leaves on forest trees.
> The thoughts of men, they still resemble
>   The air, the winds, the changeful year,
>   And the light vanes that ever veer
>   On our house-tops, and veering tremble.
> Their love no stay or firmness hath,
>   No more than billows of the sea,
>   That roar, and run, and in their wrath
>   Torment themselves continually.

His verses on Marriage, and his Adieu to Poland, prove that he could be at times sarcastic.

At p. 596, we find a sonnet on the Bergerie of Remy Belleau ; and at p. 631 another on the death of the same poet.

There are commendatory verses on Desportes himself, by the Cardinal du Perron at p. 243, and by Bertaut at p. 306 ; and in one of the elegies to his memory, at the end of this volume, with the signature, J. de Montereul (of whom I find no mention elsewhere), he is thus described :

> Open he was, frank, liberal and kind ;
> And, at his table, every Muse combined
> To greet all comers, and each day did sit
> Those throughout Europe famousest for wit.

Philippe Desportes was born at Chartres, in 1546; and died at his Abbey of Bonport, in Normandy, on the fifth of October, 1606. Charles IX presented him with eight thousand crowns for his poem of Rodomont; and for one of his sonnets he was remunerated with the Abbey of Tiron. It was a piping time for the Muses. Of the wealth which thus flowed in upon him he was as generous as his eulogist has described him. Almost all the contemporary poets were his friends; and those amongst them who stood in need of his assistance did not seek in vain.

JEAN BERTAUT

1552—1611

———

THE edition of Bertaut's poems which I met with in the old French library was entitled Recueil des Œuvres Poetiques de J. Bertaut, Abbé D'Aunay, et premier Aumonier de la Royne. Seconde edition. Paris, 1605. The reader will not expect much imagination of copies of verses written on such subjects as The Conversion of the King, The Reduction of Amiens, A Discourse presented to the King on his going to Picardy to fight against the Spaniard, A Discourse to the King on the Conference held at Fontainebleau; and there is about as much poetry in them as in those by Waller, Dryden and Addison on similar occasions. The poem on the death of Ronsard (though it has much mythological trifling about Proteus, and Nereus, and Thetis, and Jupiter, and Mercury in the shape of the Cardinal du Perron) becomes exceedingly interesting towards the conclusion, where Bertaut expresses his affection for the departed poet and the zeal which he had early felt to imitate him :

Scarce sixteen years I number'd when my breast
Was with the sacred love of song possest ;
A common doom so early I eschew'd,
And on thy steps immortal fame pursued.
Long ere my prime had ripen'd into man,
From vulgar cares with proud contempt I ran ;
Mine hours in pensive solitude were past,
And my first spring a wint'ry cloud o'ercast :
When, so it chanced, I lighten'd on the strain
Where mild Desportes essay'd his happy vein.
Love and the Muse with such a native grace
Endued his numbers that I thought to trace
A copy of them in my simple lore.
Fond that I was, who had not learn'd before
How difficult for arts like his to please,
Nor aught less easy than that seeming ease.

Once more to thee I turn'd, and thought my pain
In imitating thee would prove less vain ;
But still more desperate th' attempt to mould
Verses in brass should equal thine of gold ;
So that for ever my o'erweening skill
Had lost the hope, though it preserved the will.
Then with no books but thine my hands were
    fraught
Thee the sole boast of human kind I thought ;
Thine image in all places, at all hours,
Hovering before me, raised my drooping powers.
Thy name I honour'd, thy abode revered,
Like holy temples to the immortals rear'd,
Beholding Grecia's palm once more expand
Her sacred blossoms, foster'd by thy hand

Briefly (if I may speak so bold a word)
Thou wert become mine idol : I adored,
And in my heart thine eloquence enshrined,
Like to the Gods, or godlike of mankind.

True is, the blaze of that exceeding light,
Flash'd from thy glory on my aching sight,
Its feeble nerve o'erpowering by the ray,
Which less illumined than confused the way,
Had made me from thy train at last elope,
Scared from Parnassus ; if, the youthful hope
To follow, thou hadst not inspired again,
Giving me back the courage thou had'st ta'en.

Thou chiefly, noble spirit, for whose loss
Just grief and mourning all our hearts engross,
Who, seeing me devoted to the Nine,
Didst hope some fruitage from those buds of mine ;
Thou didst excite me after thee t'ascend
The Muse's sacred hill ; nor only lend
Example, but inspirit me to reach
The far-off summit by thy friendly speech :
Clio, thou saidst, when first my breath I drew,
Had on my cradle cast a favouring view ;
That, if I look'd to shun the grasp of Death,
I should be daring, and expend my breath
On outspread volumes : so would fair renown,
By hard exertion won, at last my labours crown.

May gracious Heaven, O ! honour of our age,
Make the conclusion answer thy presage :
Nor let it only for vain fortune stand
That I have seen thy visage—touch'd thy hand.

Meanwhile accept, if aught thou deign of ours,
These tears of anguish, which, instead of flowers,
Instead of hallow'd streams thine urn to lave,
We with all France are pouring on thy grave.

This warm and affectionate admiration of the two poets
who then divided the homage of their countrymen,
Ronsard and Desportes, does great credit to Bertaut.
His hope of being easily able to imitate the sweetness
of the latter, his failure in the attempt—his then turning
to Ronsard as his model—the encouragement given to
him by both, and the devotedness and reverence with
which he regarded everything that related to men who
in his estimation were of so great importance—all this
is told with an earnestness which makes it impossible
to doubt its truth.

There is not one other of his sonnets in the first
volume that is expressed with so much nature and grace
as the following :

To my Lord the Cardinal of Bourbon, in the name of
the inhabitants of Bourgueil.

Whilst we behold thee sojourn in a land
  Whose breast the track of livid fire hath scored,
  Compass'd about with perils and the sword,
  Nor e'en one tranquil night at thy command ;
In these fresh valleys, with unwilling hand,
  We cull the fruits in bounteous plenty pour'd ;
  On these gay lawns, amidst the vernal hoard
  Of scents and blossoms, unrejoicing stand :

Not that, to sullen waywardness a prey,
　We loathe the gifts allow'd us, by annoy
　Untainted, amidst the general misery ;
But that, while thou, O Prince ! art far away,
　Public concern permits not to enjoy
　That peace and quiet which we owe to thee.

At p. 238 of the first volume is Timandre, Poeme, contenant une tragique Aventure. This tragical adventure, intended to show the ill-effects of trusting in those who deal with familiar spirits, is related with much fluency of numbers, and a style remarkable for its familiarity and ease.

The second volume, which contains his love-poems, none but a lover could have patience to read to the end. Like those of Desportes, or of our own Cowley, they present us with the idea of no living object. The fancied mistress seems to be nothing more than a web stretched out oh the warp for the purpose of embroidering the poet's conceits ; and, of these, many are the mere sports of an idle ingenuity, which have no concern either with the imagination or the heart : such is the description of her hand :

" As to her beautiful hand, that living wonder, which renders Love the possessor of my freedom, it might be said to be without an equal in the world, if heaven had condemned it not to have a sister : but for my double misfortune it was born a twin, and both framed of a marble that is endowed with motion, and cleft into ten branches : the one is the committer of the theft, and the other its concealer ; the one perpetrates the murder, and the other defends it."

Yet it would be unjust not to own that there are some genuine touches of tenderness : as when he is about to lose the company of his mistress :

> La crainte de perdre un chose si chere
> Fait que je ne sens point l'heur de la posseder.
>
> (V. 2, p. 23.)

> I feel no bliss in having, through my fear
> To lose a thing that is so passing dear.

His regret for past happiness is expressed in some verses which, when I began to read them to an ingenious French gentleman of my acquaintance, I found were so familiar to him that he was able to go on with them, though he neither knew whence they came nor was aware that such a poet as Bertaut had ever existed.

> Oh ! pleasures gone, but ne'er forgot,
>   That still my thoughts pursue ;
> Oh, losing ye, why lost I not
>   Remembrance of you, too ?

> Alas ! of all its joys bereft,
>   My heart looks back in vain ;
> The sad remembrance only left
>   Converts them into pain.

The following stanzas will supply future commentators with a parallel passage to the well-known apothegm in Shakespeare :

Men's evil manners live in brass ; their virtues
      We write in water.

  Men's wrongs alone in mind we bear ;
    Ingratitude is everywhere :
  Their injuries we in metal grave,
    And write their kindness in the wave.

  Love can a proof of this supply,
    Who mingles pleasure with his pain :
  The good we pass in silence by,
    And only of the ill complain.

A pretty conceit of Waller's to be found in Bertaut :

  The eagle's fate and mine are one,
    Which on the shaft that made him die
  Espy'd a feather of his own,
    Wherewith he wont to soar so high.
                    Waller

  To a Lady singing a song of his composing.

  He doth of us blind homage claim ;
    In madness we his vassals are ;
  And, when his cruelty we blame,
    The fault is in our own despair.

  We only brew the bitter draughts
    On which our witless heart he feeds ;
  And our own feathers wing the shafts
    By which our wounded bosom bleeds.

> Our sloth first brings the babe to light ;
>   Our hopes his suckling nurses be :
> Our weakness giveth him his might ;
>   Our servitude his tyranny.

In one of his sonnets we have the same thought as in those stanzas of Shenstone on which Johnson has pronounced—that the mind which denies them its sympathy has no acquaintance with love or nature.

> Je meurs me souvenant que sa bouche de basme,
>   D'un baiser redoublé qui me déroba l'ame,
>   En ne disant adieu me pria du retour.

>   So sweetly she bade me adieu,
>   I thought that she bade me return.

The only poem in which I have observed anything like an attempt to describe the person of his Amarantha is termed an Elegy (p. 66), where he introduces Love appearing to him, after he had forsworn his affection for Chloris and resolved to secure himself from similar engagements by the study of astronomy. The god, in addition to his usual weapons, the bow and the quiver, has a roll of paper in one of his hands, and expostulates in a sarcastic vein with the rebel on his intentions :

> Well, young astrologer, and thou hast broke
> My bonds at last, and freed thee from the yoke !
> The valiant Hercules ! he bursts my net
> To hold the heav'ns up, and for Atlas sweat.

'Tis well : perséver : be thy youth employ'd
Counting the stars, that so thou mayst avoid
The pains of sloth ; then, all thy vigour gone,
Avoid Love's pleasures when old age creeps on.

The poet replies that the ingratitude and cruelty of
Chloris had made him resolute to persevere in the course
he had taken. On this, Love seems to allow the justice
of his plea ; but argues that he is not to give over the
chase because the prey has once escaped him ; that the
mariner who has suffered shipwreck again puts to sea ;
and the labourer, whose hopes of a harvest have failed,
still continues to commit his seed to the earth : and,
when Bertaut persists in his contumacy, ends by unfolding
the paper : this presents him with a portrait of a new
mistress, which, as might be expected, he finds irresistible.
Here there is no want of sprightliness either in the invention or the style ; but his materials are spun out
somewhat too diffusely.

Jean Bertaut was born in 1552, at Caen, in Normandy,
a province where the poetry of France may be said to
have originated under the auspices of its English sovereigns, or, to speak more properly, the Norman sovereigns
of England ; and which has since continued to support
the honours it had so early acquired. He was the First
Almoner to Queen Catherine de Medici. By Henry III
he was made Private Secretary, Reader, and Councillor
of State. Henry IV, who was induced partly by his
arguments or persuasion to conform to the Church
establishment of France, gave him the Abbey of Aunay
in 1594 ; and in 1606 appointed him Bishop of Sees in
Normandy. Besides the poems already mentioned, he

made a translation of the Second Book of the Æneid, inserted in the collection of his poems, and a translation or paraphrase of the Psalms into French verse, which is not among them, and which was perhaps not made till after he became a bishop. He died in 1611, at the age of fifty-nine.

MAURICE SCEVE

d. 1564

PASQUIER, in his Researches on France (Recherches de la France, I. 6, ch. 7), speaks of Maurice Sceve as the leader of that troop, in the reign of Henry the Second, who, deserting the vulgar and beaten track, struck out into a more retired and lofty path. " In his younger days," says Pasquier, " he had trod in the steps of the rest; but, when advanced in life, chose to enter on another course, proposing to himself for his object, in imitation of the Italians, a mistress whom he celebrated under the name of Delia, not in sonnets (for that form of composition had not yet been introduced), but in continued stanzas of ten (dixains), yet with such darkness of meaning that in reading him I owned myself satisfied not to understand him, since he was not willing to be understood. Du Bellay, acknowledging his priority in his own style of writing, has addressed to him a sonnet, in which he says :

O gentle spirit, ornament of France,
  Who, by Apollo sacredly inspired,
  Hast from the people, first of all, retired,
Far from the path mark'd out by ignorance.

And in the fiftieth sonnet of his Olive, the same poet calls him ' new swan ' ; implying that by a new method he had banished ignorance from our poetry. The consequence has been that his book has perished with him." Thus far Pasquier. It can scarcely be hoped that a modern reader should pierce through

> That double night of darkness and of shade

with which Maurice has invested his Delia, since one who was so much nearer to her orb professed himself unable to penetrate it. Yet sometimes methinks she

> Stoops her pale visage through an amber cloud,
> And disinherits Chaos ;

and it is during a few of these occasional gleams that I could wish to exhibit her.

> Love lost the weapons that he aim'd at me,
> And wail'd for woe that he his soul unmann'd ;
> Venus with pity did that sadness see,
> And sigh'd and wept till she put out her brand ;
> So did they both in grievous sorrow stand,
> Her torch extinct, his arrows spent in air.
>   Cease, goddess, cease thy mourning ; and repair
> Thy torch in me, whose heart the flame supplies ;
> And thou, child, cease ; unto my lady fare,
> And make again thy weapons at her eyes.

> When darksome hours the welkin have embrown'd,
> And sluggish Somnus lulls the world to peace,
> Buried in curtains shadowing around,
> Cometh a dream that doth my spirit release,

And in her presence bids its wandering cease,
Whom it hath reverenced for her royal guise.
  But with so soft and intimate surprise
Hers draws it on that I, unfearing soon,
Methinks am folding her ; yet in such wise
As once the Latmian shepherd did the Moon.

In another of these dixains he refers to the death of Sir
Thomas More, whose fate had then recently filled Europe
with consternation.

Soft sleep with silent waters had bedew'd
My temples in oblivion that I felt
The torch of son and mother both subdued,
And their wan fires in dark suffusion melt,
Or so believed : for by the night is dealt
Repose to mortals, stealing cares away.
  But morn stept forth ; and with that morn the day
Tack'd round, and did a thousand deaths restore ;
For virtue, whose proud zeal no let can stay,
Had to the world lost England and her More.

When to herself I of herself complain,
Making her rue the wrong that she hath done,
Her bright eyes, swelling with self-disdain,
Oft melt in dew that into showers doth run.
But, as when sometimes we do see the sun
In spring-time peering through a showery sky,
The nightingale is blithe, and curiously
'Gins warble, dewing his meek feathers still ;
  Thus in the tears that drop from either eye
Love bathes his wings, reposing him at will.

The moon at full, by clearness of her light,
Breaks through the thickness of the troublous shade,
Whose bristling horror, leagued with the night,
Has the wayfaring wanderer dismay'd ;
Then doth he onward go, no more afraid
Lest doubtful darkness lead his feet astray.
   Thus she, whose motion doth my spirit sway,
With sweet looks, sovereign cure for my distress,
Dissolves my humid cloud of grief away,
Leading me forth in shining steadfastness.

This poem, entitled Delie, Object de plus haulte Vertu, and printed at Lyons, chez Sulpice Sabon, pour Antoine Constantine, 1544, 8vo, consists of 458 dixains, reckoning by the number at the end ; but of these, nine (between 90 and 100) are omitted. Every second leaf is ornamented with some curious emblem ; and the portrait of the author is prefixed. I am the more particular in describing this book because I am doubtful whether it had ever been reprinted, and because, amidst such obscurity, there are really some fine things in it, somewhat in the way of our own Donne. Besides those which I have attempted to translate, I would direct the attention of my reader, if it should chance to come in his way, to dixains ciii, cxxv, cccxxxvii, ccccv, and ccccxxiii. In the two hundred and sixty-second, and that following it, he celebrates Francis the First ; and, in the next two, Margaret, probably the daughter of that king and Duchess of Savoy. After the quaint fashion of the times, his Delia is often accosted as the Moon. She appears to have been a married woman :

> In Francis' time,
> Such courtship was not held a crime.

He frequently speaks of the Rhone, on the banks of which he resided, probably at Lyons. Maurice Sceve himself was an advocate, and afterwards chief magistrate (echevin) in that city; and died, an old man, about 1564. Another of his works, called the Microcosme, written in Alexandrine verse, and divided into three books, I have not seen.

GUILLAUME DES AUTELS

1529—1580

———

THE only book which I have seen by Guillaume
des Autels consists of but sixteen small leaves
in the Gothic letter. It has no name of printer,
nor date of time or place ; its title, Le Moys de May,
de Guilelme Deshaultelz de Montcanis en Bourgoignes
Deus Scit (with two rude figures of a man and woman
conversing together). On the back of the title-page,
the reason why it is so called is given in the following
quatrain :

> Reader, light of heart and gay,
>   Of this title if the reason
>   Thou inquirest, know the season
> When I made it was in May.

Nearly all the next seven leaves are taken up with the
dialogue between two personages, who are called Guilelme
and Jeanne. The gentleman proposes questions (de-
mandes d'amour) and the lady resolves them. The
following will be enough to show in what manner this
catechism proceeds.

WILLIAM :   An if thou weetest, tell me this,
             And tell me sooth I pray ;
             Whence jealousy in human heart
             Did first begin to sway ?

JANE :   According to my fantasy,
             Which is not false herein,
             The cause of jealousy did first
             In love o'erstrong begin.

Then follow some epigrams, in which, though he addresses the first of them to his sister and friend, the Damoiselle Jeanne de la Bruyere, and the second to his father, there is nevertheless a licentiousness in which I suppose the writer conceived that the " sprightly month " would warrant him.

Next comes Co~plaincte sur la Mort de Cleme~t Marot p Calliope muse q' se peust cha~ter sur Laisses le verde couleur faict p ledict Deshautelz.—" Complaint on the Death of Clement Marot, by the Muse Calliope, which may be sung to the tune of ' Leave the Green Colour,' by the said Des Autels."

        Upon the top of high Parnass
          The Muses nine did sit,
      When sudden on that mount the earth
          Shook with a fearful fit.

        Thereat the quadrant toward the stars
          Did turn itself around,
      And forth there issued, mix'd with sobs,
          A song of doleful sound.

Oh, break ye off this cheerful strain,
   Oh, break ye off your gladness ;
Calliope, dear sister, we
   Have tidings of strange sadness.

Weep for the son of Phœbus, weep,
   And for his hapless doom :
This month, erewhile a happy month,
   Hath seen him to his tomb ;

Him, who had next to Virgil learnt
   His golden pen to move ;
Who made the measures nimbly trip
   In song and lay of love.

It ceased ; but only at those words
   Calliope despair'd,
For well she knew that Clement's soul
   Had from its body fared ;

And at so mighty woe disturb'd,
   Away her gladness fled ;
And, changing colour, down to earth
   She fell as she were dead.

Her sisters, beautiful and kind,
   That saw her in that swound,
With gentle care enfolded her,
   And lifted from the ground :

And when her voice, that fail'd her quite,
    A little was restored,
She thus, in accents faint and low,
    That luckless chance deplored :

Ah me ! she cried, O cruel death,
    Insensate and ill-starr'd,
Thy dart on me no wound can work,
    Ye hath it prest me hard.

Alas ! how well art thou avenged
    On me for my disdain,
Who in the place I held so dear
    Hast thy proud station ta'en.

Now is thy great ingratitude
    To all men clearly shown ;
Now is thy rude and felon hand
    Through every nation known.

He, who to utmost of his might
    Had colour'd o'er my wrong,
Has suffer'd from thy luckless hand
    In guerdon of his song.

Marot, in the discourse of the good and evil shepherd,
thus praises death :

He call'd thee bountiful and good,
    He named thee key to bliss ;
And, if they've learnt to paint thee fair,
    The lesson hath been his.

> Each limner hence that limneth best,
>   Who doth thy likeness trace,
> Describeth thee with beauty such
>   As beam'd in Helen's face ;
>
> And thou wert made thy dart to bear
>   With heaven's own azure bright,
> As courteously as Cupid his,
>   In golden quiver pight.

In the second of these stanzas there appears to be intended a play on the words quadran, the instrument, and quadrain or quatrain, a stanza of four lines. After continuing her complaint through several more of these, Calliope at last, like Gray's Bard, plunges in the Caballine stream ; but not, like him, to endless night—for her immortality does not suffer any harm in the mighty waters. Another impression of the same figures that are in the title-page, and which seem designed to represent Guilelme and Jeanne, concludes this little volume.

I regret much that I can do no more for this writer than point out the names of some of his other works from De Bure's Bibliographie : 3055. Repos de plus grand travail, ou Poësies diverses ; composées par Guill. des Autelz. Lyon, de Tournes, 1550, in 8vo.—3056. Replique du même Guill. des Autelz aux furieuses défenses de Louis Megret, en prose ; avec la suite du Repos de l'Auteur, en rime Francoise. Lyon, de Tournes, 1551, in 8vo.—3057. Les Amoureux Repos de Guill. des Autelz, avec les facons lyriques, et quelques epigrammes. Lyon, Temporal, 1553, in 8vo.—3621. Mythistoire Baragouyne de Fanfreluche et Gaudichon, trouvée depuis nagueres, d'un exemplaire écrit à la main (par Guill. des Autels.), Lyon, 1574, in 16mo.

Guillaume, son of Syacre des Autels, was born at Charolles, in 1529, and died about 1580.

ROBERT GARNIER

1534—1590

——

JODELLE'S fame, as a dramatic writer, was soon eclipsed by that of Robert Garnier, who, indeed, if we were to take the words of Dorat and of Robert Estienne (grandson, I believe, of him who compiled the Thesaurus), surpassed even the three tragedians of Greece.

> La Grece eut trois autheurs de la Muse tragique,
> France plus que ces trois estime un seul Garnier.
> R. Estienne.

> At nunc vincit eos qui tres, Garnerius unus,
> Terna ferat Tragicis præmia digna tribus.
> Jo. Auratus.

His other panegyrists, Ronsard, Belleau, Baïf, Flaminio de Birague* and Claude Binet, are more temperate; and Estienne Pasquier, after quoting Ronsard's testimony

* Flaminio de Birague lived in the time of Charles IX, and composed quatrains, sixains, sonnets, elegies and epitaphs. One of the epitaphs is cited by M. Philipon-la-Madelaine, in his Dictionnaire Portatif des Poetes Francais. Paris, 1805.

> Passant, penses tu pas de passer ce passage
> Qu'en mourant j'ai passé ? Penses au même pas,
> Si tu n'y penses bien, de vrai tu n'es pas sage ;
> Car possible demain passeras au trépas,

in his favour, and reciting the names of his eight tragedies, contents himself with adding that they will, in his opinion, find a place among posterity.* "A mon jugement trouveront lieu dedans la posterité."

In some prefatory verses to Henry III, Garnier well describes the character of these poems :

> A tragedy
> Like this which humbly I present to thee :
> Through the big verse, where blood and horrour rage,
> And tears, and sobs, and fury swell the page.

He has a tumid grandeur which frequently expands itself even beyond the dimensions of Seneca himself. Like Shakespeare, he sometimes boldly coins a word when the language does not supply him with one that will suit his purpose.

The speeches are often immoderately long. He has much declamation ; occasionally a good deal of passion ; but very little character.

In what manner he conducts his stories my reader will be able to judge from the following abstract which I have made of each of those wherein the plot is, for aught I know to the contrary, his own.

In the first, which is entitled Porcie, the fury Megæra speaks the prologue. The chorus of Roman women then sing the perils of grandeur and the safety of lowliness in an ode, much of which is from Horace.—Act 2. Porcia laments the miseries of her country. The chorus sing a translation of Horace's Beatus ille qui procul

* Recherches de la France, l. 6, c. 7.

negotiis. The nurse also mourns over the sufferings of Rome, and expresses her fears for the approaching conflict between the forces of Antony and those of Brutus and Cassius, and for the effects which the defeat of the latter may produce on her mistress. Porcia now comes in, and in her despair regrets the death of Julius 'Cæsar. The chorus again sing a moral ode, much of which is from Horace.—Act 3. Areus, the philosopher and favourite of Octavius Cæsar, makes a long soliloquy on the happiness of the golden age, and the subsequent corruption of mankind, concluding with a quotation from Horace. Octavius, who has now been informed of the death of Brutus, enters exulting, and vows further vengeance on his enemies, from which Areus endeavours to dissuade him, but in vain. There is in this scene a brisk alternation in the dialogue.

AR. Cæsar proscribed no man to sate his vengeance.
OCT. Had he proscribed them all, he yet in Rome
     Were reigning.
AR. He was sparing of their blood.
OCT. Say rather he was lavish of his own.
AR. A citizen's life was precious in his eyes.
OCT. The life of one who is a citizen,
     And loves us, ever must be dear ;
     Not his who is a citizen, and hates us.
AR. Cæsar pardon'd all.
OCT. Whereto served his pardon ?
AR. To win more to him.
OCT. What was its reward ?
AR. That graven in our hearts his glory lives
     Eternally in blest remembrance.

OCT. Yet he died.

AR. Not so his praise, which is immortal.

OCT. But for his body, is't not in the tomb?

AR. And could he 'scape to die?

The chorus sing the mutability of human affairs and the unhappy destinies of Rome. Antony and Ventidius, his lieutenant, return to Rome after their victory. Antony salutes the city in a pompous speech, and Ventidius sets him on recounting the labours of his forefather, Hercules, and boasting of his own achievements. He is joined by his two colleagues, Octavius and Lepidus, who debate on the measures to be pursued in future, and resolve to set out for their several provinces. A chorus of soldiers conclude the act.—Act 4. The messenger, after much delay and circumlocution, and many long similes, communicates the fatal tidings to Porcia, who breaks forth into the most clamorous grief.

> Thunder, ye heavens, flash, lighten, swallow up,
> Nor leave one little particle of all
> My seared bones, which this ungrateful earth
> May in its bosom cover. Pour, pour down
> Your utmost spite on this blaspheming head;
> And execute your stormy wrath so fully
> That naught remain of such a wretch as I am.

The nurse endeavours to soothe her, to no purpose. The chorus once more bewail the fate of Rome.

Act 5. The nurse relates to the chorus the death of her mistress. They lament over that event, and the fate of Brutus, in a simple and pathetic song; and the nurse concludes the play, with a poniard at her breast, in the following couplet :

> Die, die we then.   No ling'ring.   Haste thee, dagger ;
> Up to thy hilt be buried quick within me.

CORNELLIE*

Act 1.   Cicero, in a long soliloquy, deplores the servitude of Rome under Julius Cæsar, and expatiates on the mischief of ambition.   The chorus sing an ode on the wickedness and evil of war.—Act 2.   Cornelia bemoans the fate of her two husbands, Crassus and Pompey. Cicero endeavours to console, and to argue her out of her intention to commit suicide.   A fine ode by the chorus on the perpetual revolution and changes in human affairs—Rome, once freed from her kings, has been again enslaved, and will some time be in like manner restored to liberty.—Act 3.   Cornelius tells the chorus of a terrible dream, in which Pompey had appeared to her. The chorus assure her that the spirits of the deceased cannot return, but that evil demons assume their appearance in order to fill us with vain terrors.   Cicero makes another turgid soliloquy on the ambition of Cæsar. Philip (who had been the freedman of Pompey) enters, bearing, in a funeral urn, the ashes of his late master. Cornelia laments over them, and inveighs against Cæsar. Another ode by the chorus, on the mutability of fortune, concludes the Act.—Act 4.   A scene between Cassius and Decimus Brutus, in which the former excites the latter to vengeance against the tyrant   The chorus

---

* Garnier's Cornelia was translated by Th. Kyd in 1594.

sing the glory of those who free their country from
tyranny, the insecurity of kings, and the happiness of a
low condition. Cæsar and Mark Antony ; the one
exulting in his conquests, the other warning him against
his enemies. There are some splendid verses put into
the mouth of Cæsar.

> O beauteous Tyber ! and do not thy billows
>   Snort out their gladness, with redoubted curls,
>   Up their green margins mounting, all o'erjoy'd
>   At my return ? do they not hasten onwards
>   Unto the foamy sea, to tell my triumphs
>   In surging clamours, and to bid the Tritons
>   Trumpet the praises of my valorous deeds ?
>   Vaunting to Father Neptune that their Tyber
>   Rolls prouder waves than Tygris or Euphrates ?

A chorus of Cæsar's friends celebrate his praises, and
declaim on the evils of envy.—Act 5. A messenger
relates to Cornelia the defeat and death of her father,
Scipio, embellishing his tale with a due proportion
of similes. Her grief clamorous and eloquent as
usual. . . .

Cornelia concludes by resolving to live, that she may
honour the remains of the dead.

> But oh ! if death surprise me ere I lodge
> My father in his tomb, who then shall do
> That office for him ?   Shall his limbs go wand'ring
> For ever up and down the murderous waves ?
> Yea, I will live, my father—I will live,
> My husband, but to make your tombs, and weep

Upon you, languishing away my life
In pining sorrow, and bedewing still
Your noble ashes with my plenteous tears,
And then at last, for lack of moisture, falling,
Sob out my soul into the happy urns
That shall contain you ; and, an empty shadow,
Flit down among the spirits of the deep.

ANTOINE

Antony makes a speech not much in character, deploring his captivity to the charms of Cleopatra. The chorus sing an ode on the miseries incident to human nature ; for part of which they are indebted to Euripides, and to Horace for the remainder.—Act 2. Philostratus appears, for this time only, that he may lament over the state of Egypt. The chorus in their song run over all the instances of unhappy mourners whom they can recall to memory, and say they have themselves more reason to mourn than all, but do not tell us for what cause. Cleopatra, with Eras and Charmion, her women, and Diomedes, her secretary. The Queen declares her resolution to share the fate of the conquered Antony, and will listen to no arguments for consulting her own safety. She goes into a sepulchre, there to await her doom. Diomedes remains alone, to meditate on the beauties of his royal mistress, and to lament her obstinacy. The following ode predicts the subjection of the Nile to the Tyber, but suggests a topic of consolation to Egypt in the future destruction of Rome herself.—Act 3. Antony discovers to his friend Lucilius his fears of Cleopatra's fidelity. Lucilius endeavours to calm his apprehensions ; and after much empty moralizing on his own weakness, and on the fatal effects of pleasure, Antony resolves to put an end to his life. The chorus chant an Ode, partly borrowed from the *Justum et tenacem propositi virum* of Horace, in which they commend the determination of Antony and Cleopatra not to survive their misfortunes.—Act 4. Octavius Cæsar enters, boasting of his triumphs. Agrippa is dissuading him from his design of exterminating his enemies, when Dercetas comes to acquaint him with the particulars of Antony's death. His death is bewailed by Cæsar, but Agrippa thinks only of being in time to prevent Cleopatra from destroying herself and her treasures. A chorus of Cæsar's friends lament the divisions of the Roman Empire, in a song which, according to custom, is in great measure translated from Horace.—Act 5. Cleopatra, in the monument with her children, their tutor Euphron, and her women, Charmion and Eras, utters her last lamentation over the dead body of Antony.

HIPPOLYTE, LA TROADE ET ANTIGONE

The subject of these three tragedies being taken chiefly from Sophocles, Euripides and Seneca, I shall willingly decline the task of being as particular in my account of them as of the rest. In the first, the ghost of Ægeus speaks the prologue. Then comes in Hippolytus, who, in a speech of about one hundred and fifty lines, declares his foreboding of some approaching evil. Had Mr. Charles Lamb met with a similar passage in one of our old dramatists, I do not think he would have passed it unnoticed.

Already doth the goddess of the dawn
Peer forth, and ruddy Phœbus following
Makes the night torches flare ; his pawing coursers
Scatter down light on all earth's animals
That do but wait them, and the beetling cliffs
Grow amber with the chariot of God
Whom they spy coming.   O fair beaming Sun !
Bright Planet, that dost push thy subtle beams
Through the dun night ! great golden-tressed God,
Who with thy luminous wand mine eyes uncharming,
Extinguishest the errour of vain dreams,
That all this troublous night have haunted me ;
Hail to thee, Father ! and again all hail
To thee, thy car and steeds, and beams of gold.

 Methought in sleep I wander'd all alone
Through a deep forest, where I oft resort,
Into a valley, with a thousand trees,
With their tall antlers girdling, shut from day.
I stood in darkness, yet not darkness such
As in full night by slumber companied ;
But as when late at evening, after sol
Has quite withdrawn his visage, and yet leaves
A light, that seemeth neither night nor day
But both conjoin'd.   And in that shadowy vale,
Upon my right, methought there was a cave,
Moss-lined, and mantled with a shaggy vine.
Four of my dogs at random enter'd it,
Four stout Molossians of right warlike breed ;
But, scarcely had they dived into its jaws,
When a fierce lion met them.   Such a beast,
So large, so massive, and so full of dread,
Amid the wilds of Taurus never stabled.

His eyes of fire glared like two beacon torches
In a dim sky.   His big and fleshy neck,
And his wide brawny chest, were swoln and bristled
With a rough matted fell : his throat was horrible,
And horrible his teeth, within the maw
Ranged like to monstrous spikes.   My dogs, alert
And hardy as they were, no sooner spy'd him
Than they sprang out in terrour, and did run
Up to me, quaking, out of breath, and yelping
With a shrill feeble wail.   Soon as I see them
Thus cow'd, I strive to hearten them again ;
But their slack courage rallies not a jot ;
And, by how much the more I tarre them on,
They, more afear'd, recoil.   As a brave leader,
That sees his people routed, and the enemy
Dogging their heels, cries out, exhorts, persuades,
Entreats them to return and face the foe :
But bootless all ; in vain he promises,
In vain he threatens ; they have lost their daring,
Are deaf, and mute, and dream but of their flight.
I grasp my pike, whose iron tip advanced
Glistens before me, and informs my path,
Then, on the brink arriving, I perceive
The mighty lion, that with outstretch'd paws
Darts at me, uttering from open throat
So dread a roar that all the forest shook,
And from Hymettus the redoubled cry
Echoed, and on Thriasian shores the rocks
Arch'd their steep brows in wonder.   Firm I stand,
Stiffen each nerve, against a trunk my back
Prop, and, one leg outstretch'd, on either arm
Right towards him couch my pike, ready to pierce

His gorge or entrails, if he dared advance.
But he no more account had of my spear
Than if I had been armed with a straw;
Seized it, and snapp'd in twain; then suddenly
Upset me under him, drags on, and rolls me
As easily as he had done a ball.

Already were his clutches in my breast,
Ripping me up like to a tiny bird
That from his mother's wing a kite hath ravish'd
And rends in pieces with his murderous claws;
When, by the torment vanquish'd, I so loud
Shriek'd out that I broke off my dream, and, waking,
Leap'd up, so chill, so trembling, and so frozen
My face, and arms, and body were but ice.

Thus on my bed long time I lay extended
Gazing around me like a man distract,
Who, reft of thought, and memory, and sense,
Wots neither what he is, nor better knows
Other beside himself; a motionless clod,
And heap of mere confusedness within.

Nor this, alas! the whole of what I fear,
Or that doth fill my spirit with strange boding
Or of some unknown event. I have a heart
Too stout to be the prey of a false dream.
This is not all that frays me; for a dream
Should not itself be cause of our annoy;
Since 'tis no more than a vain empty shadow,
And so presagement of the thing to come.
These four or five nights past, the owlet ne'er
Hath ceased lamenting on our palace roof;
And, soon as in their kennel stall'd, my hounds
Howl like to forest wolves. Our castle towers

Are black with ravens, perched night and day ;
Sepulchral birds, that will not quit their seat,
Though driven, save when I go forth to hunt ;
And then it seems as all took wing at once
From the steep battlements, and, croaking round me,
Accompanied my steps this way and that,
Flapping their dismal pennons in mid-air,
Self-balanced, like a thick and low-hung cloud.

The lively song of the attendant sportsmen tends to
dispel these horrors.   It must be owned that there is
something in all this more to our English taste ; in short,
that it has more of character and of picturesque effect
than the opening of Racine's Phèdre, in which the tutor
of Hippolytus is trying to extort from his pupil a confession of his being enamoured of Aricia, which a little
prudery alone restrains him from avowing.

Il n'en faut point douter, vous aimez, vous brûlez,
Vous périssez d'un mal que vous dissimulez.
La charmante Aricie a-t-elle sû vous plaire ?
HIPPOLYTE : Théramene, je pars, et vais chercher,
mon pere.

The young prince, though a votary of Diana herself,
if he had not had a mistress would have appeared more
savage than any of the wild beasts he hunted, in the eyes
of that court, where, as Voltaire tells us, the prime
minister himself could not be without one.   In the next
scene the judgment of Racine led him to follow Euripides,
though he has done it most timidly, and with a sacred
horror of the bold and passionate imagery of the Greek.

In his preface, acknowledging his obligations to that writer for the conception of Phædra's character, he tells us that he believed he had never exhibited anything so reasonable on the stage. " Quand je ne lui devrois que la seule idée du caractere de Phèdre, je pourrois dire que je lui dois ce que j'ai peut-être mis de plus raisonnable sur le théatre." And to her reason indeed it must be allowed he has brought her in the strait-waistcoast of his Alexandrines ; for the poor queen raves no more as she had formerly done in her palace at Athens about dewy dountains, pure waters, poplars, tufted meadows, pine trees, beast-slaughtering hounds, spotted stags, and Thessalian spears ; about Diana mistress of the sea-lake, and Venetian horses ; but talks as a lady might be supposed to talk who had lived the greater part of her life at Paris, and was subject to be at times a little flighty.

> Dieux, que ne suis-je assise à l'ombre des forêts ?
> Quand pourrai-je, au travers d'une noble poussière,
> Suivre de l'œil un char fuyant dans la carrière ?

Garnier would assuredly have made more of this ; but he has unfortunately struck off into the route of Seneca, who makes the queen speak of her love for Hippolytus in the presence of the nurse as if the latter were already acquainted with it, and so loses one of the finest occasions ever offered to a dramatic poet to show his art in the casual and unconscious discovery of an illicit passion. The " Ah, Dieux ! " of Racine's Phædra on the mention of the name of Hippolytus is not equal to the οἴμοι of Euripides. It does not sound so much like a moan drawn from the bottom of a heart ready to burst with a sense of its sufferings. In the rest of the play, Garnier has not departed far from Seneca's model. Euripides alone introduces Hippolytus still alive at the conclusion, and has a short but moving scene between him and Theseus.

In the preface to the Troade, Garnier owns that he has taken it partly from the Hecuba and Troades of Euripides, and partly from the Troas of Seneca. It is by expansion that he is most apt to spoil the effect of what he borrows. In Seneca, Andromache, when she is begging of Ulysses to spare the child Astyanax, says :

> An has ruinas urbis in cinerem datas
> Hic excitabit ?

And then, holding up his little hands, adds :

> Hæ manus Trojam erigent ?

than which scarcely anything can be imagined more pathetic.* But, when Garnier makes four words into as many lines, it is dilated almost to nothing.

> Quoy ? ces floüettes mains, ces deux mains enfantines
> Pourront bien restaurer les Troyennes ruines ?
> Pourront bien redresser les meurs audacieux
> De cendreux Ilion, que battirent les Dieux ?
>
> (p. 352.)

An Italian poet, Bongianni Gratarolo, who has treated

---

* " The master-piece of Seneca," says Dryden, in his Treatise on Dramatic Poesy, " I hold to be that scene in the Troades, where Ulysses is seeking for Astyanax to kill him. Then you see the tenderness of a mother represented in Andromache."

the same subject in his Astianatte, manages it much better.

> Son queste mani da redrizzar Troja ?   (Act 4.)
> And are these hands to build up Troy again ?

In like manner, when Talthybius relates to Hecuba the sacrifice of Polyxena, Garnier has enlarged on the narration in Euripides, which, beautiful as it is, is yet sufficiently long.

Into his Antigone he has crowded much of the Septem Contra Thebas of Æschylus, the Phœnissæ of Euripides, and the Thebais of Seneca ; nor is it till the fourth act that he takes up the subject as it is treated in the Antigone of Sophocles.   The farewell of the heroine, when she is about to enter her living sepulchre, will be well remembered by all readers of that master of the drama.   It is thus imitated by Garnier :

> O fontaine Dircee ! ô fleuve Ismene ! ô prez !
> O forests ! ô costaux ! ô bords de sang pourprez !
> O soliel jaunissant lumiere de ce monde !
> O Thebes, mon pays, d'hommes guerriers feconde
> Et maintenant fertile en dure cruauté,
> Contrainte je vous laisse et votre royauté !
>
> .   .   .   .   .   .
>
> Hà, je scay que bientost sortant de ma caverne,
> Je vous verray, mon pere, au profond de l'Averne !
>
> .   .   .   ,   .   .
>
> Je vous verray, ma mere, esclandreuse Iocaste,
> Je verray Eteocle, et le gendre d'Adraste,
> N'agueras devalez sur le noir Acheron,
> Et ne passez encor par le nocher Charon.

Adieu, brigade armée ; adieu, cheres compagnes,
Je m'en vay lamenter sous les sombres campagnes :
J'entre vive en ma tombe, où languira mon corps
Mort et vif, esloigné des vivans et des morts.

(p. 478.)

Instead of a translation of these lines I will add an
attempt which I once made to compress the original into
a few Latin elegiacs.

Hos viva Antigone, jamjam subitura sepulchrum,
   Thebas respiciens, fudit ab ore sonos.
Sancta vale sedes, comitesque valete puellæ,
   Et tu Dircæi fluminis unda vale.
Nunc licet extremûm patrias insistere terras ;
   Nunc licet extremo munere luce frui.
Intereo misera, amplexûs ignara mariti :
   Turbavit pompas mors, Hymeneæ, tuas.
At nec pœniteat vitales luminis oras
   Linguere, et inferni visere regna Dei ;
Sic cari potero vultus agnoscere fratris,
   Sic umbræ occurrent ora paterna meæ.
Adsum, clamabo ; generisque miserrima nostri,
   Fato Labdacidæ stirpe creata probor.

The subject of the next tragedy, entitled Les Juiffes,
the Jewish women, is taken from the Bible (II Kings,
xxiv, xxv. Act 1). The prophet deplores the defeat of
the Jews. The chorus sing a hymn on the fall of man
and on the deluge.—Act 2. Nebuchadnezzar, after an
arrogant speech, equalling himself to the Almighty,
declares to Nebuzaradan, captain of the guard, his intention to punish with death the rebellion of the King

of the Jews, from which that officer in vain endeavours to dissuade him. A chorus on the mischiefs resulting from the Jewish connection with Egypt. Hamutal, mother of Zedekiah, bewailing her desolate condition, with the Jewish women.

> Will there not come a day, when I may whelm
> In the dark tomb my sorrows, made the prey
> For worms ? Alas ! I think, 'twill never come ;
> Long time it is since I call for 't in vain,
> In vain expect it. Oh ! my pains are lasting.
> E'en death, the general helper, helps not me.
> Trembling he flees away, nor ventures near me :
> His dart, that knows no terror, dares not touch me,
> He fears the evils that enclose me round ;
> Or thinks I dwell immortal in this world,
> Sent by God's wrath to wander up and down
> Within this place of torment as my hell.

The Assyrian Queen commiserates her misfortunes, and tries with much delicacy and tenderness to comfort her. The chorus sing a farewell to their native country. —Act 3. While the Queen is interceding with Nebuchadnezzar for the Jews, Hamutal and the wives of Zedekiah enter ; and, at their supplications, the Assyrian King at length makes a treacherous promise of mercy. The chorus sing a hymn from the psalm " By the Waters of Babylon, etc."—Act 4. Seraiah, the chief priest, represents to the King of the Jews, when he is bewailing the sins and calamities of himself and his people, that nothing is left him but to submit with tranquillity and fortitude to the Divine dispensations. Nebuchadnezzar

now enters, and reproaches them with their rebellion.
At first, Zedekiah acknowledges his offence, but is afterwards irritated into defiance by the brutality of his conqueror. The chorus in a hymn remember with anguish
their former happiness, and contrast it with their present
sufferings. The master of the household to the Assyrian
king comes to demand the royal children from Hamutal
and the wives of Zedekiah. The chorus sing the perpetual instability of fortune.—Act 5. The Prophet
announces to Hamutal and the Queen the cruel murder
of the children, whom they had given up as hostages to
Nebuchadnezzar. Zedekiah then enters with his eyes
put out; and the Prophet concludes the tragedy by
foretelling the deliverance of the Jews by Cyrus, the
rebuilding of the temple, and the coming of Christ.

BRADAMANTE

The last of Garnier's plays, which is entitled a tragi-
comedy, and has no choruses, was suggested, as the author
says in his preface, by the latter part of the Orlando
Furioso. In this he has conducted the plot much more
artfully than in any of the rest.—Act 1. Sc. 1. Charlemagne is introduced exulting over the delivery of his
kingdom from the forces of Agramant.—Sc. 2. Nymes,
Duke of Bavaria, advises him to be content with his
victory, and not to pursue further the remains of his
routed enemies. The King expresses his design to reward
his faithful soldiers, and especially Roger, by uniting him
in marriage and Bradamante, whom her parents, Aymon
and Beatrix, designed for Leon, son and heir to Constantine, the Grecian Emperor; but in order to secure her

for her lover, and at the same time not to contradict
openly the will of her parents, Charlemagne intends
that she shall be the prize of the knight who shall vanquish her in single combat.—Act 2. Sc. 1. Aymon
and Beatrix hold a conversation on the intended marriage
of their daughter. There is something comic in the
pleasure with which they express their hopes of getting
her off their hands without a marriage-portion to the
Emperor's son.—Sc. 2. Renaud expostulates with his
father on his resolution to force a husband on his sister
Bradamante. The old man falls into a rage, threatens
to fight all who oppose his will, and calls to his servant,
La Roque, for his arms, at the same time that he can
scarce stand for feebleness.—Sc. 3. Beatrix strives to
wheedle her daughter Bradamante into the match with
the Emperor's son. One of the verses that are put into
her mouth on this occasion being a good translation of the
patria est ubicunque bene est, has I think passed into a
proverb :

Le pays est partout on l'on se trouve bien.

Bradamante parries her mother's attempt very artfully,
and alarms her so much by saying that she will turn nun
that the old lady consents to her marrying Roger.—
Act 3. Scene 1. Leon, who had fallen violently in
love with Bradamante from the mere report of her beauty,
arrives at Paris in the company of Roger, whom, although
his enemy, he had freed from prison ; and whom (not
knowing him to be his rival) he now engages to undertake
for him the single combat which Charlemagne had
proposed. Roger's gratitude does not allow him to deny
the prince this request, though his granting it will lose

him his mistress.—Scene 2. Bradamante, in a soliloquy, laments the absence of Roger.—Scene 3. Relying on the prowess of his friend, who is to counterfeit him, Leon speaks confidently of his own success to Charlemagne, who promises that he will be as good as his word, and give Bradamante to him if he shall conquer her.—Scene 4. Bradamante, with her attendant, Hippalque, in the presence of Charlemagne, declares her contempt of the " debile Gregois," the " jeune efféminé," who aspires to win her hand in the duel ; and her resolution to have no husband but her old lover.—Scene 5. Roger enters alone, disguised in the armour of Leon ; and, distracted between his love on the one hand and his obligations tò his friend on the other, determines at last that he will meet Bradamante in the list, but that he will exert himself no further than to parry her weapon.—Scene 6. Bradamante, too, comes on the stage alone. She makes a fine speech on French heroism, and resolves to give her young antagonist no quarter.—Act 4. Scene 1. La Montage, who had been present at the single combat which is supposed to have taken place since the last Act, gives a lively description of it to Aymon and Beatrix, who rejoice at the defeat of their daughter, not doubting but she will now be compelled to espouse Leon.—Scene 2. Roger, in an agony of despair, imprecates curses on his own head for having lost his mistress by conquering her for Leon.—Scene 3. In equal grief at her own defeat, Bradamante professes to her friend Hippalque that she will die rather than fulfil her engagement, and bitterly laments the supposed absence of Roger.—Scene 4. During their conversation, Marphise, the sister of Roger, comes in, and Hippalque devises a plan, which is eagerly caught at, for deferring the proposed nuptials till Roger's return. It is that Marphise shall represent to Charlemagne the wrong that is done to her brother in his absence; shall charge Bradamante with being secretly betrothed to him, and with having deserted him for her royal suitor; and shall offer to maintain the accusation by a trial at arms; that Bradamante shall pretend confusion at this challenge; and that, in the mean time, Charlemagne will no doubt be induced to suspend the proceedings.—Scene 5. The plot is put into execution, and the result is that Roger, as soon as he makes his appearance again at Paris, is to fight Leon.— Scene 6. Leon proposes to employ Roger, whom he does not yet know to be his rival, to extricate him from this new difficulty; but is informed by Basile, Duke of Athens, that his friend is no longer to be found in Paris.— Act 5. Scene 1. Leon, who meets with Roger, now discovers who he is, enters into a contest of generosity with him, and insists on yielding Bradamante to him.— Scene 2. Meanwhile the ambassadors of Bulgaria having arrived at the court of Charlemagne announce that their countrymen had elected Roger for their new king, in recompense of his having defended them against the Greeks.—Scene 3. Charlemagne acquaints Aymon with the honour conferred on Roger, and thus removes the principal objection to his union with Bradamante.— Scenes 4, 5, 6 and 7. The whole of the preceding events are explained to the satisfaction of all parties; the lovers are made happy; and Charlemagne satisfies Leon for the loss of his mistress by giving him his own daughter, Leonora.

Robert Garnier, born at La Ferté-Bernard, 1534, died

at Mans, lieutenant-general of that town. He gained the prize at the Jeux Florau ; and, in addition to the plays here spoken of, was the author of several other poems which I have not seen.

ALAIN CHARTIER

1386—1458

———

WHEN Margaret of Scotland, Dauphiness of France, was passing through an apartment in which Alain Chartier lay asleep, she went up to him and kissed him. The custom of claiming a new pair of gloves on such occasions was probably not then in use; for the ladies and gentlemen who attended her expressed their wonder that she should honour so ugly a fellow with that token of her affection; and Margaret replied that she was tempted, not by the beauty of Alain's lips, but by the golden sayings that had proceeded from them. It is painful to think that so free and gracious a lady should have died of grief occasioned by calumnious imputations on her virtue. Male Bouche, as the fiend was then called, never did the world a worse turn. But the tears of her husband, who was afterwards King of France, with the title of Louis XI, sufficiently, as Henault observes, vindicated her memory.

Alain Chartier, who was secretary to Charles VII, father of Louis, was a good poet for his day, or, rather, he was an excellent rhymer; for he will often go on with such a string of like endings that it would have posed Touchstone, in spite of his brag that he could rhyme you so eight years together, dinner and supper and sleeping hours excepted, to keep pace with him. " Grand poete de son temps, et encor plus grand orateur " is the eulogium left him by Estienne Pasquier. His Curial and Quadrilogue, the works which, in Estienne's opinion, entitle him to the praise of being a great orator, would in these days have appeared in the shape of two dry political pamphlets ; but, in those, they assumed the more inviting form of as many visions. In the first of them, the Curial, Alain, while he is musing on the decline and disasters of France, is suddenly seized by Melancholy, a doleful and squalid female, who, without speaking a word, wraps him in her mantle and casts him into a bed where three other females present themselves. These are Indignation, Distrust and Despair, whose persons are described. Indignation first endeavours to disgust him with the court ; next Distrust represents to him the forlorn condition of France ; and, lastly, Despair tempts him to seek a refuge from his sufferings in death.

" And thou, why are thou fain to keep watch on this evil mischance, and to live on, wishing for death all thy days ? The chivalry of thy land is destroyed and gone ; studies are routed ; the clergy are dispersed and oppressed ; the rule and government of ecclesiastical decorum is turned with the time into disorder and dissoluteness. The citizens are disfurnished of hope, and inobservant of seignory, through the darkness of this thick cloud ; order is changed to confusion, and law into unmeasured violence ; just seignory and honour are fallen out of their place ; obeisance is wearied out ; patience fails ; everything is going headlong into the abyss of ruin and desolation."

He is ready to listen to the suggestions of Despair, when Nature, alarmed at the thoughts of dissolution, is so violently agitated that she rouses up Understanding, who was sleeping by his side. Understanding opens the wicket of Memory, the bolts of which had been held fast by the rust of Forgetfulness : by this three ladies and a very fair damsel immediately enter. The first of these, who is Faith, addresses Understanding, and resolves many doubts which are proposed to her by that personage. Here he takes occasion to inveigh most bitterly against the abuses which had crept into the Church.

" Dante, poet of Florence, thou, if thou wast still living, wouldst have cause to cry out against Constantine ; seeing that in a time when religion was better observed thou wert yet bold to reprehend, and didst reproach him, for having infused into the Church that venom and poison wherewith he should be wasted and destroyed." (Fol. 36.)

Soon after he speaks with a mixture of pity and anger concerning the persecutions which the poor clergy in Bohemia. had lately undergone ; becomes eloquent in his indignation against those by whom the churches had been violated ; and reproaches the French people with their degeneracy since the days of Charles the Fifth. Deeper questions are afterwards discussed. Hope explains to Understanding in what manner human passions and perfections were attributed to the Deity, and endeavours to reconcile the free-will of man with the foreknowledge of God.

She next declares in plain terms the enormity that had been occasioned by the celibacy of the clergy, and the other crying sins which were then imputable to the Church. The other two ladies, whom he had before introduced, do not continue the conversation, as might have been expected; and the Curial ends abruptly with a warning addressed to the author's brother against the life of a courtier. In this book there are short poetical pieces interspersed, very inferior to the prose.

He tells us that the unhappiness of his country, and the desire of recalling his fellow-citizens to a sense of their duty, were the motives which induced him to write the Quadrilogue, so named from the four persons who are represented speaking in it. Dame France appears to him about the dawn of day—a noble lady, but full of sorrow, and dressed in " wondrous hieroglyphic robe." She addressed her three sons, under whom are figured the populace, the nobility, and the clergy, and descants on the miseries to which they, in conjunction with foreign enemies, had reduced her. They mutually criminate each other. France puts an end to their debates by exhorting them to concord, and by desiring that their several pleas may be committed to writing, a task which she orders Alain to undertake.

Puis que Dieu ne ta donne force de corps, ne usage d'armes, sers la chose publique de ce que tu peux. Car autant exaulca la gloire des rommains, et renforca leurs courages a vertu la plume et la la~gue de leurs orateurs, comme les glaives des combatans. (Fol. 139.)

" Since God hath not given thee force of body or skill in arms, serve thy country in that thou mayest ; for the glory of the Romans was as much advanced, and their courage as much invigorated by the pen and tongue of their orators as by the swords of their warriors."

The Belle Dame sans Merci of this poet is known to us from a translation inserted by some mistake among the works of Chaucer, who died when the Frenchman was about fourteen years of age. Tyrwhitt says that in the Harleian manuscripts, 373, the version is attributed to Sir Richard Ros. Whoever the author of it may be, it is very well done ; and sometimes surpasses the original, as in the following stanza :

> De puis je ne sceuz quil devint
> Ne quel part il se transporta
> Mais a sa dame nen souvint
> Qui aux dames se deporta
> Et depuis on me rapporta
> Quil avoit ses cheveulx descoux
> Et que tant en desconforta
> Quil en estoit mort de courroux.   (Fol. 199.)

Fro thens he went, but whither wist I naught,
Nor to what part he drew in sothfastnesse,
But he no more was in his ladies thought,
For the daunce anon she gan her dresse,
And afterward, one told me thus expresse,
He rent his heer, for anguish and for paine,
And in himselfe toke so great heavinesse
That he was dedde within a day or twaine.

(Fol. 243.   Speght's Edit., 1602)

Here it is evident that the translator must have made use of a manuscript of Chartier's works more correct than the edition of 1529; for, instead of dames in the fourth line, he has translated as if it were danses, which was, no doubt, the right reading. In another place, this edition of Speght appears to be faulty.

> De ceste fest je lassay
> Car joye triste coeur travaille
> Et lors de la presse passay
> Si massiz dessoubz une traille
> Drue et fueillie a grant merveille
> Entrelardee de saulx vers
> Se que nul pour cep et pour fueille
> Ne povoit parveoir au travers.
>
> (Fol. 188.)

> To see the feast it wearied me full sore,
> For heavy joy doeth sore the heart travaile ;
> Out of the prease I me withdrew therefore,
> And set me down alone behind a traile,
> Full of leaves to see a great mervaile,
> With greene wreaths ybounden wonderly
> The leaves were so thick withouten faile
> That throughout no man might me espie.
>
> (Fol. 239.)

Instead of wreaths, the word was probably withs. The second line, which, in the original, conveys the natural sentiment that " Joy is trouble to a heart in sorrow," was evidently misunderstood by the translator.

The introduction to the Livre des Quatre Dames, written in 1433, is a lively picture of a spring morning, so much in Chaucer's way that one might suppose it had been copied by that writer, if the images were not such as the poets of the time most delighted to assemble. The four ladies severally lay their griefs before Alain. The first had lost her lover, who was killed at the Battle of Agincourt; the lover of the second had been made prisoner; that of the third was missing, and of the fourth had run away.

The poem that approaches nearest to the sprightliness of old Geoffrey is the Hospital d'amours, if that be indeed Chartier's, but it is a little strange that he should speak of himself as being interred in the cemetery of the hospital, as he does in these words:

" Near, at the end of a path, lay the body of a very complete wise and loyal person, Alain Chartier, who did many a fine feat in love, and make known the misdeed of her by whom her lover was slain, and whom he called, when he had made that poem, La belle Dame sans Mercy. Round about his tomb in letters of gold was all the art of rhetorick engraven."

The following verses, being one of his seven ballads on Fortune, may give a fair view of his character as a poet:

On lake of mourning by the stream of woe,
Full of loud moans and passionate distress,
By melancholy fountain dull and slow,
Full of sad tears and sobbings comfortless,
By a great pond surnamed of bitterness,

And fast beside the abyss of grief profound,
There Fortune ever doth her dwelling found
Upon a hanging ledge of rock unstable,
Th' unsurest spot that may in earth be found,
Shewing to all that she is never stable.

One part is bright, the other most obscure,
Of that some dwelling made for mortals vain :
One side is rich, the other mean and poor ;
Here stretcheth wide a bare unsightly plain,
And fields are there that wave with fruits and grain.
So Fortune sits abounding all in air,
On one side black, on th' other white and fair ;
On one part sound, on th' other perishable,
Mute, deaf, and blind, as all her deeds declare,
Shewing to all that she is never stable.

And there in place held by her proud right hand,
That scorneth bit or bridle to retain,
In her dread dwelling there doth ever stand
Conceal'd of dire mishaps a monstrous train ;
To beat down sin with well-deserved pain,
And worldly might and glory to confound ;
For at one turning of her great wheel round
She of a palace makes forthwith a stable,
More swiftly than a swallow skims the ground,
Shewing to all that she is never stable.

What will ye more ?   This is the sum of all :
If Fortune smiles at one time favourable,
She bringeth at the next a grievous fall,
Shewing to all that she is never stable.

It may be worth while to observe that many of the Chaucerian words are to be found in Alain Chartier, and that he will sometimes assist us in putting the right signification on them. For instance, the word *tretis* is explained in Tyrwhitt's Glossary, *long and well-proportioned*, though it is plain, from a passage in the Regrets d'un Amoureux, that the French word from which it is derived cannot bear that meaning.

Sa petite bouche et traictise. (Fol. 325.)

Alain Chartier was born in 1386, and died in 1458.

CHARLES,
DUKE OF ORLEANS

1391—1466

——

IT is now (in 1823) but a few years since the first
publication of some French poems, written at
the beginning of the fifteenth century, which
not only excel any other of that time that we are
acquainted with, but might at any time be regarded
as patterns of natural ease and elegance. What makes
this long neglect the more difficult to account for
is that the author of them was a prince, grandson
to one of the French kings, father to another, and uncle
to a third; the first (Charles V), renowned for his wisdom; the next (Louis XII), for his paternal care of his
subjects; and the third (Francis I), for his courtesy,
and his love of letters. When we are told that the
writings of a person thus distinguished had been so long
suffered to remain in darkness, it is natural to suspect that
some imposition may have been practised on the public
respecting them. But there is no ground for such
suspicion. They have not been discovered by some
apprentice boy, in an old church coffer, like the poems
of Rowley, not by the son of a prime minister, in some
other out-of-the-way place, like the Castle of Otranto.
The manuscript which contains them was noticed in the
Royal Library at Paris, near a century back, by the

Abbé Sallier, who inserted three papers on the subject in the Memoirs of the Academie des Inscriptions.* Another, from which the publication was made, is in the public library at Grenoble ; and, to put the matter out of doubt, a third, of singular splendour, is to be seen in our own national library of the British Museum. The last of these was once the property of Henry VII of England, whose daughter Mary was married to the son of the poet himself, the above-mentioned Louis XII.

The Abbé Sallier remarks that if Boileau had seen these productions he would not have called Villon the restorer of the French Parnassus. I am not sure of this. The palate of Boileau required something more poignant. In these there is as much simplicity as in some of Wordsworth's minor pieces. The chief difference is that these are almost all love verses.

> In dream, and wish, and thought, my Love,
>   I see thee every day ;
> So doth my heart to meet thee move
>   When thou art far away.

> For that all worldly joys above
>   Thou shinest in thy array ;
> In dream, and wish, and thought, my Love,
>   I see thee every day.

* Tome xiii, p. 580, Tome xv, p. 795, and Tome xvii, Mars 1742. In the first of the Abbé's papers here referred to, the manuscript in the Royal Library at Paris is thus described. It had belonged to Catherine of Medicis. The arms of Charles, Duke of Orleans, impressed on the first leaf, together with those of Valentina, of Milan, his mother, shewed that Catherine had got it from the library of her husband, Henry II. It contained 131 songs, and about 400 rondels ; and, lastly, a discourse pronounced before Charles VII, in favour of John II, Duke of Alençon.

No care, no hope, no aim I prove
  That is not thine to sway :
Oh ! trust me, while on earth I rove,
Thy motions I obey,
In dream, and wish, and thought, my Love.

      (Poesies de Charles d'Orléans, p. 208.
                  Paris, small 8vo. 1809.)

To make my lady's obsequies
My love a minster wrought,
And, in the chantry, service there
Was sung by doleful thought ;
The tapers were of burning sighs
That light and odour gave ;
And sorrows, painted o'er with tears,
Enlumined her grave ;
And round about, in quaintest guise,
Was carved : " Within this tomb there lies
The fairest thing in mortal eyes."

Above her lieth spread a tomb
Of gold and sapphires blue ;
The gold doth shew her blessedness,
The sapphires mark her true :
For blessedness and truth in her
Were livelily portray'd,
When gracious God with both his hands
Her goodly substance made :
He framed her in such wond'rous wise
She was, to speak without disguise,
The fairest thing in mortal eyes.

No more, no more : my heart doth faint
When I the life recall
Of her, who lived so free from taint,
So virtuous deem'd by all :
That in herself was so complete
I think that she was ta'en
By God to deck His paradise,
And with His saints to reign ;
For well she doth become the skies,
Whom, while on earth, each one did prize
The fairest thing in mortal eyes.

But naught our tears avail, or cries :
All soon or late in death shall sleep :
Nor living wight long time may keep
The fairest thing in mortal eyes.

One day it chanced that in the gloomy grove
Of sorrow all alone my steps I bent ;
So met I there the mother queen of love,
Who call'd me, asking whitherward I went.
Fortune, quoth I, in exile hath me sent
Within this wood long time to weep my woes :
Well mayst thou name a wight so sorely shent,
The wilder'd man that wots not where he goes.

She smiled, and answer'd in her lowliness :
Friend, if I knew why thou dost hither stray,
Thee would I gladly help in thy distress
In the best manner that in sooth I may :

For erst I put thy heart in pleasure's way ;
Nor aught I ken from whence thy grief arose,
It irketh me to see thee here to-day,
The wilder'd man that wots not where he goes.

Alas, quoth I, my sovran lady dear,
Thou knowst my hap : what need I tell it thee ?
Death, that doth reave us of all treasures here,
Hath taken her who was a joy to me,
Who was my guide, and held my company,
In whom I did my only hope repose,
Long as she lived ; not fated then to be
The wilder'd man that wots not where he goes.

I am a blind man now, fain to explore
With staff outstretch'd this way and that before,
Feeling the path that none unto me shows.
Great pity 'tis I must be evermore
The wilder'd man that wots not where he goes.

The Time hath laid his mantle by
Of wind and rain and icy chill,
And dons a rich embroidery
Of sun-light pour'd on lake and hill.

No beast or bird in earth or sky
Whose voice doth not with gladness thrill,
For Time hath laid his mantle by
Of wind and rain and icy chill

River and fountain, brook and rill,
Bespangled o'er with livery gay
Of silver droplets, wind their way:
So all their new apparel vie;
The time hath laid his mantle by.

In blinking at the bonny flowers
When April them to love doth woo,
And all shine brighter in the bowers,
And all are deck'd with colours new;

No heart there is but youth restores
Amid their breath of balmy dew,
In blinking at the bonny flowers,
When April them to love doth woo.

The birds are dancing in their glee
Upon the twigs mid blosmy showers;
There sing they loud in their chauntrie
Counter and tenor merrily,
In blinking at the bonny flowers.

The life of Charles, Duke of Orleans, might furnish the materials for a romance, or rather for several romances. He was born on the 26th of May, 1391. His father, Louis, Duke of Orleans, the second son of Charles V, was married in 1389 to Valentina, daughter of the Duke of Milan. After the death of Charles, France was distracted by factions. The minority of his son, Charles VI, made it necessary that a regency should be appointed.

His four uncles contended for this distinction. The King had not long been of age when the frequent fits of lunacy to which he was liable again made him incapable of ruling except only at intervals. His brother, Louis, now put in his claim to a share in the government, and in the disputes which ensued between him and two of the uncles, the Dukes of Berri and Burgundy, Louis was assassinated by the orders of the latter in the Rue Barbette at Paris, on the 23rd of November, 1407. A formal and feigned reconciliation took place at Chartres in a year or two after between the families of the murderer and the murdered; but Valentina died of grief at seeing the death of her husband unrevenged. A tissue of odious intrigues is entangled with these horrors. The Duke of Burgundy was supposed to be partly instigated by jealousy of his wife to the commission of his crime, for which there was the less excuse as that very wife was the favourite of the King, as he himself was the paramour of the Queen, the infamous Isabel.

At the age of sixteen, Charles of Orleans had married a daughter of this King and Queen, of the same name with her mother, and widow of Richard II of England. In three years after (1409) his consort died. Thus before the age of twenty he found himself not only orphan but a widower. A second marriage with Bonne, daughter of the Count of Armagnac, involved him in new troubles. The Count had put himself at the head of a faction opposed to the Duke of Burgundy, and from him called the Armagnacs. A short truce for a while suspended these differences; till the Count de Saint Pol, who was Governor of Paris, determined on driving out of the capital all those who were not in the interest of the Duke of Burgundy, and for that purpose united a band of 500 bravoes, who were called the Cabochiens, from Caboche, a butcher, one of the principal amongst them. In an evil hour, either Charles of Orleans or his father-in-law sought assistance from the English.* The consequence of this ill-advised measure was the Battle of Agincourt, in which it so happened that the Duke himself fell into the hands of the invaders ; for the King of France had in the meantime declared against the Duke of Burgundy, and Charles was therefore now fighting on the side of the King against those very enemies whom he had himself invited. In the field of Agincourt he was found lying amongst a heap of slain, with some signs of life in him, by a valiant soldier, of the name of Richard Waller, who brought him to Henry V. Waller being desired by that monarch to take charge of his prisoner, on their return to England, confined him in his own mansion at Groombridge, near Tunbridge, in Kent. This misfortune did not come alone, for at the same time he lost his second wife, Bonne of Armagnac. How long he remained in Waller's custody is not known ; but he had time enough to rebuild the house that was assigned for his habitation. His piety also led him to contribute to the repairs of the neighbouring church of Speldhurst, over the porch of which we are told by the historians of the county that the arms of the Duke carved in stone are still to be seen.† From John, the second son of this

* In the paper by the Abbé Sallier, inserted in the Memoires de l'Academie des Inscriptions, tom. xv, p. 795, are some curious particulars of an embassy by Jacques le Grant into England, sent by the Orleans or Armagnac party.

† See Harris's " History of Kent," vol. i, p. 292, and Hasted's " History of Kent," vol. i, p. 431

Richard Waller, were descended the Wallers of Becons-
field, of whom I conclude the poet Edmund to have been
one.

Before the eighth year of Henry VI, as Hasted, in his
History of Kent informs us, the Duke had been committed
to other custody; for it was that year enacted in Parlia-
ment that the Duke of Orleans, the King's cousin, then
in the keeping of Sir Thomas Chamberworth, Knight,
should be delivered to Sir John Cornwall, Knight, to be
by him safely kept.   There is even some doubt as to the
time which his captivity in this country lasted; but the
best accounts, I think, make it twenty-five years in all.
During this time he acquired such a taste for our language
as to compose some verses in it.   The Abbé Sallier
mentions his having written only two short pieces in
English; but in the manuscript of his poems in the
British Museum I have found three.*   They are as
follows.   I give them, not as being particularly good,
but because any verses written in our language by a

* A large collection of English poems attributed to Charles,
Duke of Orleans, is among the Harleian MSS. in the British
Museum (No. 682); they were printed by Mr. Watson Taylor
for the Roxburgh Club, in 1827, as appears by an article on these
poems in the *Gentleman's Magazine* for May, 1842, p. 459.   The
writer of that article is mistaken, he says: "We have only to
add that the opinion of Sir Thomas Croft that the English
poems now printed in the Roxburgh volume are not by Charles,
but are translations from his French poems by another bard,
is not, as far as we can learn, received by the learned in these
matters"; for in the *Collection des Documens inédits sur
l'histoire de France*, p. 70 (4to Par., 1835), it is observed of this
MS.: "Ce manuscrit contient la traduction Anglaise de la
plupart des poésies de Charles d'Orleans, executée par un con-
temporain.   L'on n'y trouve rien qui puisse autoriser à croire
qu'elle soit du prince lui-même; ainsi M. Watson Taylor, qui a
publié ce recueil, n'a-t-il aucune raison solide à apporter pour
justifier le titre qu'il lui a donné, titre que nous avons rapporté
ci-devant."—ED.

foreigner at so early a time, that is, very soon after the death of Chaucer, may be regarded as a curiosity.

> Go forth, my hert, with my lady;
> Loke that ye spar no bysines
> To serve her with such lolyness,
> That ye gette her oftyme prively
> That she kepe truly her promes.
> Go forth, etc.

> I must, as a helis body,
> Abyde alone in hevynes;
> And ye shal dwell with your mastris
> In plaisaunce glad and mery.
> Go forth, etc.

By helis body, I suppose is meant one deprived of health or happiness. The word occurs in Chaucer, but with a difference in the spelling and quantity.

> A wight in forment and in drede
> And healelesse.
>> (Troilus and Creseide,
>> Book V, fol. 180, Ed. 1602.)

> My hertly love is in your governa~s,
> And ever shal whill that I live may.
> I pray to God I may see that day
> That ye be knyt with trouthful alyans.
> Ye shal not fynd feyning or variaunce
> As in my part; what wyl I truly say.
> My hertly, etc.

Bewere, my trewe innocent hert,
How ye hold with her aliauns,
That somtym with word of ples~ns
Resceyved you under covert.
Thynke how the stroke of love comsmert*
Without warnyng or deffiauns.
Bewere my, etc.

And ye shall pryvely† or appert
See her by me in loves dauns,
With her faire femenyn contenauns
Ye shall never fro her astert.‡
Bewere my, etc.

From these strains it would appear as if the young
widower had been smitten by some English lady during
his long abode amongst us. Soon after his release,
he married Mary, Princess of Cleves, by whom he had
one son, Louis XII of France, and two daughters, Mary,
the wife of Jean de Foix, Vicomte de Narbonne, and
Joan, Abbess of Fontevrault. He had another daughter
by his first wife, who was also named Joan, and was married to the Duke of Alençon. Among those who most
joyfully welcomed his return to his native country was
his illegitimate brother John, the brave Count of Dunois,
by whom the English were expelled from Normandy.

On the death of Filippo Maria Visconti, Duke of
Milan (in 1447), Charles made an ineffectual attempt to

---

* Query, for can smart, or comes smart.
 † Prive and apert is in Chaucer, Cant. T. 6696. In private
and in public, Tyrwhitt's Glossary.
 ‡ Astert. Chaucer Cant. T. 1597, 6550. To escape, Tyrwhitt's
Glossary.

recover that inheritance in right of his mother, who was sister to the Duke.

At the accession of Louis XI to the crown of France, he was so mortified by the dissimulation of that monarch that he retired in disgust from the court. He died on the first of January, 1466, in his 75th year.

Besides his poems and the speech delivered in favour of the Duke of Alençon, there are remaining some of his letters, addressed to the " good cities " of France, or to the King. They are dated from Gergeau sur Loire, July 14th, 1411, and are thus described by Juvenal des Ursins, who refers to them in the History of Charles VI. " Lettres longues et assez prolixes, et faites en fel et doux langage."*

The writer of a memoir, prefixed to his poems, adds that his tomb, which was in the chapel of Celestines, at Paris, has escaped the ravages of time and of the Revolution, and is to be found in the depository of French monuments, in the Rue des Petits Augustins.

---

* See the paper by the Abbé Sallier. Memoires de l'Academie des Inscriptions, t. xvii. Mars, 1742.

FRANCOIS VILLON

1431—(?)

———

THE praise bestowed by Boileau on Villon, and still more the pains taken by Clement Marot, at the instance of Francis the First, to edit his poems, would lead us to expect great things from them; but in this expectation most English readers will probably be disappointed. For while Alain Chartier is full as intelligible as Chaucer, and Charles Duke of Orleans more so, Villon (who wrote after both) can scarcely be made out by the help of a glossary. Even his editor, Marot, who, as he tells us in the preface, had corrected a vast number of passages in his poems, partly from the old editions, partly from the recital of old people who had got them by heart, and partly from his own conjectures, was forced to leave several others untouched, which he could neither correct nor explain. One cause of the difficulty which we find in reading Villon is assigned by Marot, in a sentence that shows his knowledge of the true principles of criticism. "Quant à l'industrie des lays qu'il feit en ses testamens pour suffisamment la congnoistre et entendre, il faudroit avoir esté de son temps à Paris, et avoir congneu les lieux les choses et les hommes dont il parle; la memoire desquelz tant plus se passera, tant moins se congnoistra icelle industrie des ses lays dictz. Pour ceste cause qui voudra faire une œuvre de longue durée, ne preigne son soubject, sur telles choses basses et particulieres." Les Œuvres de Francois Villon, à Paris, 1723, small 8vo. " As to the address with which he has distributed his legacies in the poems called his Wills, to understand it sufficiently one should have been at Paris in his time, and have been acquainted with the places, the things, and the persons of whom he speaks ; for, by how much more the memory of these shall have been lost, so much less shall we be able to discover his dexterity in the distribution of these bequests. He who would compose a work that shall last ought not to choose his subject in circumstances thus mean and particular."

The truth is that Villon appears to have been one of the first French writers who excelled in what they call badinage, for which I do not know any adequate term in our language. It is something between wit and buffoonery. Less intellectual and refined than the one, and not so gross and personal as the other, in reconciling it in some degree neutralizes both. To an Englishman it is apt to appear either ridiculous or insipid ; to a Frenchman it is almost enough to make the charm of life.

One of the chief causes of Villon's popularity must, however, have arisen in the great number of French families whom he has mentioned in his two Wills, generally for the purpose of ridiculing certain individuals who belonged to them. A list of these, containing upwards of eighty names, is prefixed to these two poems.

His " Petit Testament," which was written in 1456, he supposes to have been made on the following occasion. Being heartily tired of love, and thinking there was no other cure for it but death, he represents himself as determined on leaving this world, and accordingly draws up his will.

His "Grand Testament" was framed in a more serious conjuncture. In 1461 he was committed to prison at Melun, together with five accomplices, for a crime the nature of which is not known. But, whatever it were, he intimates that he was tempted into it by his mistress, who afterwards deserted him. He remained in a dungeon and in chains, on an allowance of bread and water, during a whole summer, and was condemned to be hung; but Louis XI (who had then newly succeeded to the throne), in consideration, as it is said, of his poetical abilities, mercifully commuted his punishment into exile. He is, perhaps, the only man whom the muse has rescued from the gallows. The hardships he had suffered during his confinement brought on a premature old age; but they taught him, he says, more wisdom than he could have learned from a commentary on Aristotle's ethics.

> Travail mes lubres sentimens
> Aguisa (ronds comme pelote)
> Me monstrant plus que les commens
> Sur le sens moral d'Aristote.
>
> (Ib., p. 14.)

"Trouble has sharpened my lubberly thoughts (before as round as a bullet), showing me more than the comments on Aristotle's Ethics could have done."

The first place at which he found a refuge was St. Genou, near St. Julien, on the road leading from Poitou into Bretagne. Here he was reduced to such extremity that he was forced to beg his bread ; and, if the fear of his Maker had not restrained him, he declares he should have put an end to himself.

There is little known of what happened to him afterwards. He probably met with some lucky turn of fortune ; for Rabelais mentions his having been in favour with Edward IV of England, and his dying at an advanced age.

From what has been said of the peculiar vein of his genius, the reader will perceive that it is scarcely capable of being fairly represented in another language. His happy turns of expression, smart personalities, and witty innuendoes, would tell very indifferently at second hand. A short ballad out of the Grand Testament, being more general, may be attempted.

Ballad of the Ladies of the Past Times

Tell me where, or in what clime,
Is that mistress of the prime,
Roman Flora ? she of Greece,
Thais ? or that maid so fond,
That, an ye shout o'er stream and pond,
Answering holdeth not her peace ?
—Where are they ? Tell me, if ye know ;
What is come of last year's snow ?

Where is Heloise the wise,
For whom Abelard was fain,
Mangled in such cruel wise,
To turn a monk instead of man ?

Where the Queen, who unto Seine
Bade them cast poor Buridan?
—Where are they? Tell me, if ye know;
What is come of last year's snow?

The Queen, that was lily fair,
Whose songs were sweet as linnets' are,
Bertha, or she who govern'd Maine?
Alice, Beatrix, or Joan,
That good damsel of Loraine,
Whom the English burnt at Roan?
—Where are they? Tell me, if ye know;
What is come of last year's snow?

Prince, question by the month or year;
The burden of my song is here:
—Where are they? Tell me, if ye know;
What is come of last year's snow?

While he was under sentence of death he wrote some
verses in which there is strange mixture of pathos and
humour. They begin thus:

O brethren, ye who live when we are gone,
Let not your hearts against us harden'd be;
For, e'en as ye do pity us each one,
So gracious God be sure will pity ye,
Here hanging five or six of us you see;
As to our flesh, which once too well we fed,
That now is rotten quite, and moulder ed;
And we, the bones, do turn to dust and clay:
None laugh at us that are so ill bested,
But pray ye God to do our sins away.

The epigram on himself, when he was condemned, is more ludicrous.

> Je suis Francois (dont ce me poise)
> Né de Paris, empres Ponthoise,
> Or d'une corde d'une toise
> Scaura mon col que mon cul poise.

Let us hope that it was no heinous offence for which he could suffer with so much gaiety.

The Petit Testament is very short, not much more than 200 verses. In the drollery, such as it is, of this fancied disposal of property, made with no other view than that of raising a laugh at the legatees, he has had a crowd of imitators. The Grand Testament, besides many items of the same kind, includes several ballads and rondels, which one of his commentators not unreasonably supposes to have been written separately, and afterwards classed under this common title, for they have no apparent connection with the main subject.

His other writings consist chiefly of a few ballads in the language l'Argot, or, as we should call it, slang. Clement Marot found them unintelligible, and left them to be expounded by Villon's successors in the art of knavery. I have not heard that any of them have undertaken the task. Indeed it would be a betrayal of their secrets, as little for their common good, as if a Romish priest were to translate the invocation of the Saints, or a physician his recipes, out of the Latin into the vernacular tongue. Of the Repuës Franches, which has been sometimes attributed to him, it is decided that he is not the author, but the hero.

Villon was born at Paris, in 1431, of mean parentage, as appears from the following stanza in his Grand Testament :

> Poor am I, poor have always been,
> And poor before me were my race :
> No wealth my sire possess'd, I ween,
> And none his grandsire, hight Erace :
> Poortith our steps doth ever trace :
> O'er my forefathers' humble graves
> (The souls of whom may God embrace)
> No crown is hung, no sceptre waves.

The time of his death is not known.

FRESNAIE VAUQUELIN

1535—1606

—

I T is one strong mark of difference between the
poets who wrote under the Valois race of kings
and those under the Bourbons that the former
have much more of individual character than the latter.
Fresnaie Vauquelin is an instance of this among many
others.   He lived, indeed, a few years after the accession
of Henry IV, the first of the Bourbons, but he belongs
properly to the Valois.   His name is now scarcely known ;
yet his works may be read with pleasure, if it were for
nothing else than the insight they give into his manners,
his way of thinking and his fortunes in life, for he was
no common man.

At a very early age he wrote and published his Foresterie, in which he boasts more than once he was among
the first to set his countrymen the example of mingling
verse with prose.

. . . toutefois dire j'ose.
Que des premiers aux vers j'avoy meslé la prose.

Les Diverses Poesies du Sieur de la Fresnaie Vauquelin
(A Caen, par Charles Macé, Imprimeur du Roy,
1612, small 8vo., p. 90, and p. 621.)

Some years after, in a bookseller's shop, he accidentally met with this juvenile production, which he had supposed to be lost (p. 621). In the Idyl, addressed to Saint Francois, Bishop of Bayeux, where the incident is mentioned, he speaks of his intending to reprint it. I know not whether he ever did so, nor whether any copy of the first impression is yet remaining. His volume of poems, to which I have referred, is closely printed, and consists of the Art Poetique, in three books ; Satires, Idyls, Epigrams, Epitaphs, and Sonnets. His Art Poetique, or Art of Poetry, is more than three times as long as Boileau's. It was undertaken at the command of Henry III, to whom at the end he addresses it in a few modest verses that contrast strongly with the rhetorical flourish sounded by Boileau at his conclusion to Louis XIV.

> These strains preceptive I for Gallia sung,
> When you, Sire, quitting Poland's harsher tongue,
> Wish'd, as beneath your laurels you recline,
> With a new grace our language to refine,
> Well pleased to hear the muse recite her tale
> In the loved leisure of your cloister'd pale.

It must sound something like profaneness to a Frenchman to hear these two writers spoken of together, yet I would venture to say that with all Boileau's good sense and flowing numbers there is very little to be found in his Art of Poetry which had not been said quite as well before by Horace ; and that, rude as Vauquelin may appear in the comparison, he gives us at least what we have some right to expect in a French Art of Poetry, more information concerning the vernacular poetry of France.

I shall notice a few particulars of this sort, which are the more remarkable as coming from a writer of his time.

He claims for the Troubadours or Provençal poets the invention of the sonnet.

These minstrels went with dance, and song, and sport,
Through every province to each prince's court.
The art, recover'd thus from Greece and Rome,
First gain'd in joyful France another home.
From their example Petrarch learnt to chime
With no new round the Sonnet's varying rhyme.
In recompense he keeps remembrance due
Of Raymond, Arnault, Rambauld, Fulk and Hugh ;
But trod so deftly in their ancient trace
He gave the Sonnet a peculiar grace.
And hence doth Italy her claim advance
To that which owes indeed its birth to France.

He then proceeds to compliment Ponthus de Thiard, Maurice Sceve, Saint Gelais, Bellay, Ronsard, Baïf and Desportes. His zeal for the honour of his country leads him yet further in the following lines :

Thus are the tongues of Italy and Spain
Vassals to our Provence and Catalaine ;
And darling Petrarch his chief honour won
From that sweet verse he learnt at Avignon.
And learned Bembo from Sicilia owns
His country took the rhyme's alternate tones,

Which thither first our old romancers bore
When Gallia's Normans sought the fruitful shore :
Conquering, they bade the Troubadours rehearse
Their feats of prowess, which in answering verse
Their own rude jugglers gave them back again,
And wandering fablers caught the heroic vein.

Another species of poems, called the Syrventez, which
he claims for the Provençals, will be more readily con-
ceded to them than the sonnet, which is now generally
allowed to be of Italian origin.

" And as our French in Provence first brought the
amorous sonnet to perfection, before the Italians, so
were they the inventors of the satirical poems, which
they then called Syrventez or Sylventois, a name that
in our sequestered forests took its origin from the sylvæ
of the Romans."

Gray, in his Observations on English Metre, speaking
of the Italian Terza Rima, observes that it was probably
the invention of the Provençals, who used it in their
Syrvientes (or Satires), whence the Italians have commonly called it Serventes.*

Vauquelin considers the verses of eight feet as best
adapted to French comedy. His account of the Alexandrine metre is the same as that which is commonly given.

" Our long verses they call Alexandrines, because the
Romance which recounted the exploits of Alexander

* Works of Thomas Gray, 2 vols., 4to, London, 1814, vol.
ii, p. 21.

the Great, one of the nine worthies of the age, was written in this measure."

The old Romances of the French, he observes, had been returned to them by the Italians and Spaniards, like a stolen horse that has had his mane trimmed and his tail and ears cut, and is then sold to the right owner for a new one. (P. 73.)

He recommends to the French poets the occasional use of provincial words, a licence at which the whole court of Louis XIV would have shuddered (p. 13); but the advice is afterwards qualified. (P. 71.)

In speaking of the tragic writers, he mentions his having been present at the representation of Jodelle's Cleopatre. (P. 76.)

The manner in which he describes the difference between the ode and the song has, I think, been imitated by Boileau. (P. 23.)

In one point he differs widely from Boileau, and that is that he earnestly recommends sacred subjects for poetry, whereas Boileau is as urgent on the other side, and would have his disciples confine themselves to the heathen mythology. A strong religious feeling is indeed one of the most striking features in the character of this poet. What shall we say to his presentment of the evils which were afterwards to befall his country from the prevalence of atheism ?

> And shall these wild excesses, France, infest
> Thy noble sons, and shake their firmer breast ?
> A threat'ning presage, that some direful storm
> One day shall far and wide thy realm deform,

As erst in Greece !   Avaunt, ye baser crew,
That rob the Eternal of his honour due.
O France, what vile ingratitude were thine
(On whom not only doth the radiance shine
From Socrates derived and Plato's page,
Those lights vouchsafed to a less favour'd age,
But that thrice blessed Gospel, which of yore
Saint Denis brought from Athens to thy shore)
If thou thankst not thy Maker, who hath graved
This holy doctrine in the heart he saved.

In the satire addressed to his poetical friend, Ponthus
de Thiard, Bishop of Chalons, he speaks with much
freedom of the enormities that prevailed among the
higher orders of the clergy, whose luxury, avarice and
ambition he considered as the chief cause of the evils
which had arisen from the Lutherans.

To his piety was joined its proper accompaniment,
a manly and independent spirit that would not suffer
him to comply with the arbitrary maxims of the day.
Amongst other hindrances to his advancement at court,
he mentions it as one :

I could not tax one Brutus for the deed
That from a Tarquin's pride his country freed,
Nor so commend great Cæsar, as to blame
The second patriot of that noble name.

In his satires he has borrowed largely from Horace
and Ariosto. From the eighth satire of the latter he has
got that ludicrous but licentious tale which Prior copied

in his Hans Carvel (p. 363) ; from his third satire, the
lively story of the magpie (p. 208), and a good deal more ;
this among the rest :

> The nightingale but ill endures the cage :
> The linnet and the finch live longer there :
> But in one day the swallow dies of rage.

To the " Beatus Ille " of Horace he is indebted for the
mould into which he has cast a very pleasing description
of the life of a French country gentleman (p. 223), and
to his Epistles (50, i. 7) for the story of the weasel (p. 232).
I take these as the first instances that occur to me of his
numerous imitations.

He complains bitterly of the little esteem in which the
best verses were held in his time :

> Since now our great men give the preference
> To a rich sausage or a ham from Mentz
> O'er all the bard can offer who in vain
> May strive to soothe them with his dulcet strain :
> For more they prize a pear, sweet bergamot,
> Or jargonel ; a luscious apricot ;
> Marchpane, or biscuit nicely baked, by far,
> Than the most perfect measures of Ronsard.

I take parpudelle, which is not found in the French
glossaries, to be the name of some fruit known in Normandy, where Vauquelin lived. The word marzepain,
marchpane, is also to be observed as being employed
by our own writers of that age, though the French
lexicographers have it not. In one of his Idyls (p. 590),

he repeatedly uses the exclamation " off, off " in the same manner as we do.

Like the rest of his poetical brethren, he everywhere acknowledges the supremacy of Ronsard, though Malherbe, who introduced a new style, had by this time got a great name. I remember one place, though I cannot refer to it, where he thus distinguishes them :

La douceur de Malherbe, et l'ardeur de Ronsard.

The satire addressed to Scævole de Sainte Marthe (p. 173) contains an interesting view of their early friendship and studies, when they strayed together on the banks of the Clain ; his regrets for the quiet and innocence of the past, and his impatience of the chicanery in which the profession of the law had engaged him. In that preceding it, he described himself as glad to escape from Caen, where his legal employment usually confined him, and to wander in the woods and listen to the nightingales beyond Falaise.

> Je ne pourroy jamais estre à mon aise
> Si bien souvent traversant par Falaise,
> Je ne quittoy de Caen le beau sejour,
> Pour mieux ouir de rossingols l'amour
> Dedans nos bois, visiter nos ombrages,
> Et les detours de nos sentiers sauvages :
> Et remarquer des Peres anciens
> L'innocent âge en nos Parroissiens.
> (Satire à Monsieur de Tiron, p. 163,

The first satire of the fifth book is very animated. At the conclusion of it he unexpectedly passes to the gay and pleasant.   In the next but one, addressed to Monsieur de la Boderie (p. 391), the miseries of the war with the Huguenots are depicted with a strong pencil and much feeling   The last of the satires, to Bertaud, the poet, gives an affecting account of the author's state of mind, occasioned by the condition to which France was then reduced.

Regnier is the only Frenchman whom Boileau has thought worthy of being enumerated among his predecessors in the art of writing satire.   It would have been no disparagement of his own dignity if he had vouchsafed a word of Vauquelin.   He might, at least, have said of him what Horace did of Lucilius :

> Ille velut fidis arcana sodalibus olim
> Credebat libris ; neque, si malè cesserat, usquam
> Decurrens aliò, neque si bene : quo fit ut omnis
> Votivâ pateat veluti descripta tabellâ
> Vita senis.

> In him as certain to be loved as seen,
> The soul stood forth, nor kept a thought within.
> (Pope.)

But it is on his Idyls that this writer should rest his pretensions as a poet.   They are often touched with a light and delicate hand.   In the preface to them he had in his simplicity laid down a definition of the Idyllium, at which one cannot help smiling.   He says it represents Nature " en chemise."   I am sorry to say he has not always left her even this slight covering, and that there are things from which a stricter eye must turn aside. Enquiring once of a young and amiable French scholar, who seldom went without a volume of Plato, or some book of divinity, in his pocket, which of the modern poets were accounted the best, I was told that Parny was the one who excelled all others in elegy. Accordingly on my next visit to Paris I got a Parny, but had not turned over many leaves before I charged my informant with having recommended to me a book that was not fit to be read. His answer was that Parny was not at all worse than some of the Greek and Latin poets, whom he knew no scholar scrupled to read; and I could plainly perceive that he thought there was something of puritanism in the objection. I could not, however, agree with him in ranking his favourite modern among such good company. The voluptuousness of Parny is covered with a veil of sentiment that renders it more dangerous than theirs. They have no fine art of seduction. Their grossness is too palpable to slide into the mind unperceived. So it is also with Vauquelin. He is not rotten at the core. His lovers, in spite of all their excesses, are still, as he calls them, " fermes et loyaux amants ! "

But I have no thoughts of entertaining my reader with anything in this way. To the following (the 77th Idyl of the first book) no exception can be made.

Shady valleys, tumbling floods,
Crystal fountains, lofty woods,
Where Philanon hath often prest
Loved Phillis to his panting breast,

Blessed be ye : never air
Of winter strip your branches bare ;
Lovely valleys, parching heat
Never soil your green retreat :
Never hoof or herd uncouth,
Fountains, break your margin smooth :
Streams, your windings never die
By the dog-star scorch'd and dry :
Nor ever woodman's axe intrude,
Forests, on your solitude :
Nor the wolf be ever here
To scare your flocks with nightly fear :
But still the Nymphs, a holy quire,
To your haunts for peace retire :
And Pan himself, with you to dwell,
Bid his Mænalun farewell.

There is something very like this in Fletcher's
Faithful Shepherdess,* which I think Warton has commended as conveying images more natural and more
proper to this country than Milton's imitation in the
Comus.

The three last Idyls of this book are religious. The
concluding one is addressed to Phillis (who it appears
was his own wife), after a union of forty years. I have
compared his version of Virgil's first Eclogue (p. 534)
with part of it translated by Malfilatre (who was also a
native of Caen) and by Gresset ; and am persuaded
that he has caught the tone of the Mantuan better
than those moderns.

---

* But the scene of the Faithful Shepherdess is laid in Thessaly.

A sonnet in praise of Virgil, or rather of two brothers of the name of Chevalier, who had translated Virgil, will not so well stand the comparison with that by Angelo Costanzo, from whom he has borrowed it.

Amongst his epitaphs are found inscriptions for Budæus ; Paulus Jovius ; the poet Marullus ; Pico da Mirandola ; la Peruse ; Tahureau* (a poet of those times whom he has celebrated elsewhere) ; Bellay ; Belleau ; Dorat ; Ronsard ; Baïf ; Toutain (another poet who lived at Falaise, and died about 1586) ; Roussel (whose excellence in Latin poetry he has highly extolled in his Art Poetique, p. 105, and who was a lawyer at Caen) ; Charles IX ; the two brothers Chevalier, who translated Virgil ; N. Michel (a physician, a Greek and Latin poet), and Garnier.

Thirty-three of his sonnets are on a young lady accidentally burnt to death at a festival at Rouen. The concluding sonnets are on sacred subjects. Among these there is one fine one on the star in the east (p. 741).

From one of his Satires (p. 181), written in his forty-fifth year, we collect the following particulars concerning this poet. He was born in the year when Francis I conquered Savoy, that is, in 1535. His family name was perhaps derived from the Val d'Eclin, then corrupted to Vauc-Elin, where his ancestors had lived. They followed William the Conqueror into England, as their names left in Gloucester and Clarence, and their armorial

* Jacques Tahureau was born at Mans in 1525, and died here in 1555. I have not seen any of his productions, which are said to consist of odes, sonnets and facetious dialogues.

achievements to be found in those places, testified. They afterwards intermarried with many noble families in France, the names of which he recounts. His father died at thirty years of age, and left him an only child and heir to an estate deeply involved, which his mother freed from all encumbrances. He was sent for his education to Paris, where he studied under Turnebus and Muretus. He knew Baïf, adored Ronsard, and honoured du Bellay, with whom he was better acquainted. In his eighteenth year he made an excursion in the company of Grimoult and Toutain to the banks of the Loire, the Sarte and the Mayenne ; in Angers, he saw Tahureau ; and, in Poitou, Sainte Marthe ; both of whom he speaks of with much enthusiasm. He now wrote his Foresterie, as has been before mentioned ; but soon after deserted his poetical studies for the law, married a virtuous lady, and succeeded to a good property that had belonged to her father. During the troubles of France he was employed confidentially by the governors of the province (Normandy), chiefly on the recommendation of Desportes. He was of moderate stature ; of a disposition somewhat jovial, bald, a little inclined to be choleric but soon pacified. This is what he tells of himself. He was afterwards made president of a court of judicature, called the Présidial, at Caen ; and died in 1606. Like our Congreve and Gray, he had no ambition to be known as an author.

De tout temps j'ay häy de Pöete le nom,
N'estant assez scavant pour avoir ce renom.

(P. 308.)

In the preface to his satire, written a little before his death, he speaks with contempt of the antithetic and pointed style which had lately grown into esteem in France.

AMADIS JAMYN

1538—1578

———

IT is entertaining enough, after reading the poems of Ronsard, to look into those of Amadis Jamyn, his page, who has quite as much of the airs of his master as one in that station ought to have. In imitation of his master he has three mistresses, after whom he names three of his books (there are five books in all)—Oriana, christened after the mistress of Amadis of Gaul; Artemis, and Callirhoe. Like Ronsard, he pays his compliments in verse to the French monarchs, Charles IX and Henry III ; the former of whom, I believe, appointed him his secretary. Through great part of the first book he is lavish in his encomiums on these princes, particularly on Charles, whom he praises equally for his wisdom, poetry, beauty and courage. The Poeme sur la Chasse au Roy Charles IX, being an animated description of the chase, may be read with more pleasure than the rest of these pieces of flattery. Like Ronsard, he dresses himself out in patches that he has purloined from the Greek, Latin and Italian poets. His best things indeed are translations ; such are those from Horace : at fol. 68, O navire dans la mer ; fol. 69, Où où mechans vous ruez-vous ainsi ? ; fol. 95, L'aspre Hyver se deslie au gracieux retour ; fol. 111, Une horrible

tempeste a ridé tous les cieux ; from Petrarch, at fol.
138, En quelle idee estoit l'exemple beau.* ; and fol. 148,
Fleurs, campagnes et prez que vous estes heureux.†
There is a pretty description of a valley, into which he has
transplanted the flowers and the nymphs from Theocritus.

> There sprang each herb of scent or colour fine,
> Green maidenhair and bluish celandine,
> The tufted parsley and lush meadowsweet,
> And many a nymph a choral round did beat
> Amid the waters, footing it amain ;
> The sleepless nymphs, dreaded by shepherd swain ;
> Eunice, Malis, and Nycheia fair
> As springtime.

He has at times even a livelier flow of numbers than
Ronsard ; but he has not near the same depth, learning
or variety. I have seen only a few lines extracted from
his translation of the Iliad and Odyssey. They have
his usual freedom and facility of verse. More might
have been said for him if he had left many such productions as the following sonnet :

> When I behold a football to and fro
> Urged by a throng of players equally,
> Who run pell-mell, and thrust and push and throw,
> Each party bent alike on victory :
> Methinks I see, resembled in that show,
> This round earth poised in the vacant sky,
> Where all are fain to lay each other low,
> Striving by might and main for mastery.

* In qual parte del ciel, in quale idea.
† Lieti fiori, e felici e ben nate erbe.

The ball is filled with wind : and even so
   It is for wind most times that mortals war ;
   Death the sole prize they all are struggling for :
And all the world is but an ebb and flow ;
   And all we learn, when as the game is o'er,
   That life is but a dream, and nothing more.

Amadis Jamyn died in 1578.

PIERRE GRINGORE

d. 1545

—

I AM half inclined to hand over Pierre Gringore to the lovers of the Gothic letter. There are three of his volumes before me, which would probably have great attractions for them. Their titles are as follows :

1. Les Abus du mõde. Nouvellement Imprimes à Paris. 8vo. (No date.)

2. Contreditz du Prince des Sots autrement dit Songecreux. On les vend à Paris en la rue neufue nostre dame lenseigne sainct Nicolas. The table of contents is wanting at the conclusion of this copy, and with it the date also, which according to De Bure is 1530.

3. Notables enseignemẽs Adages et proverbes faitz et composez par Pierre Gringore dit Dauldemont Herault darmes de hault & puissant seigneur monsieur le Duc de Lorraine, Nouvellemẽt reveuz et corrigez. Avecques plusieurs austres adjoustez oultre la precedente Impression. On les vend a Lyon cheulx Olivier Arnoullet. 16mo. 1538.

Du Bure gives the titles of twelve more of these

treasures, and on one of them, for its rarity the most precious of all, he expatiates at great length. It is No. 3269 in his catalogue, and is called Le Jeu du Prince des Sots et Mere Sotte, mis en rime Francoise; par Pierre Gringore, ou Gringoire; et joué par personnaiges, aux Halles de Paris, le Mardy gras de l'année, 1511, in 16 gotiq. From the account given of it, it appears to have been a sort of comedy, or rather farce, divided into four separate parts. A copy of it, preserved in the King's Library at Paris, is said to be the only one then known. I have not discovered whether a Duessa has since appeared to dispute the homage paid to this Una. In the Bibliotheca Parisiana, No. 252, there is at least a manuscript copy of it.

Besides all these, there is yet another book attributed to Pierre, which is not in black letter, and which in De Bure, No. 3036 with an asterisk, is erroneously said to bear the name of Octavien de St. Gelais in the title-page, unless indeed the title-pages of all the copies were not the same. This is Le Chasteau de Labour, auquel est contenu ladresse de richesse, et chemin de pouurete. Le faintises du monde. Imprime à Paris pour Galliot du Pre, 1532. 8vo.

After a prologue setting forth the author's design, he thus enters on his subject :

" In the fair pleasant garden, filled with trees, herbs and flowers, I saw a lovely young child enjoying the sweet odours. Dame Youth presented him many a floweret of divers hue. Of sorrow there was no thought, but all was pleasure and gladness. Near him was Chastisement, a master of a school of honour, who remonstrated with him gently, as a teacher with his scholar. He told him that one who labours not lives like a brute beast. The young child sets himself with good heart to listen to the words of Chastisement."

Jeune Enfant, in spite of his good advice, gets into many difficulties, which are described as allegorical personages, and some of them touched not without spirit.

The dress of Jeune Enfant himself is thus painted :

> Yclad in a green mantle gay
> Of newly fangled gore was he,
> As gent as in a popingay
> That sits in springtide on the tree.

Here we have four Chaucerian words in as many lines : " gore," " gent," " popingay," and " renouvelle." The first of these gave Tyrwhitt some trouble to explain. He does not seem to have been aware of the manner in which the old French writers used it. It occurs again in this poem.

> Vit venir ung homme de nom
> Abille en gorre nouvelle,
> Et tenoit ce gentil mignon
> Par le main une damoyselle.

> Gorrierement le saluerent
> Et il leur rendit leur salut.

(Fol. 8.)

La femme met l'homme a raison,
Il luy fault riches paremens,
En gorre selon la saison.

(Fol. 19.)

Favin, in his Théatre d'Honneur, tom. i, p. 714 (as quoted by Roquefort, in the Glossary of the Romance tongue), gives the name of Grande Gorre to Isabeau, of Baviere, " pour se bobander en habits à l'Allemande "— " from her flaunting in clothes made after the German fashion."

The last verses I have cited are in the description which Franc Arbitre, Free-Will, gives the Jeune Enfant of a wife, when he is obstinately bent on marriage. Marry, however, he will; and, as the lady proves a " Grande Gorre," " a lady of fashion," according to Franc Arbitre's prediction of her, the difficulties of Jeune Enfant are thus completed. When he is ready to sink under them there appears to him a lady, quite another sort, who delivers him out of them all. This is no less than the Blessed Virgin, whom the author calls also " Reason."

At the beginning of the French Revolution, the philosophers thought they were freeing themselves from all their old superstitions when they worshipped, in the person as it is said of a common woman, the Goddess of Reason; though they were, in fact, relapsing into a very old superstition, only stripped of all that was decorous and affecting to the imagination. The Virgin, or Reason, gives Jeune Enfant some excellent advice, which is further enforced by the admonitions of a grave old man, called " Entendement," " Understanding ";

but all is like to prove of no avail in consequence of the
arrival of one who comes up dressed in the garb of a
lawyer.

> This lord of whom I spake was clad
> In likeness of an advocate ;
> On head a cope of fur he had,
> And trail'd behind a robe of state.

This is " Barat," " Barrateria " Ital. " Baratry " in
our old law language, accompanied by his clerk, " Tri-
cherie," " Treachery," and his valet, " Hoquellerie,"
" Chicanery." " Hoker " and " Hokerly " are words
in Chaucer, which, as well as our word " Hukster," are
probably of the same stock with this. This goodly
trio are endeavouring to seduce Jeune Enfant from his
duty, but their ill-intentions are defeated by " Reason,"
who is reinforced by a man and woman in plain garb,
the one named " Bon Cueur," the other " Bonne
Voulente "—" Good Heart " and " Good Will "—bringing with them " Tallent de bien faire "—" Desire of
Well-doing." These lead him to the castle of Labour.
" Peine," " Pain," the lady of the castle, enquires of
" Soing," " Carefulness," the porter, who drew the new-
comer in and from whence?

> Vient il d'Angeleterre ou de Romme ?
> (Fol. 77.)
> " Comes he from England or from Rome ? "

He declares his willingness to be employed, and
" Peine " tells him that her husband " Travail," " Work,"

will see how he executes his task, and reward him accordingly. He has much to do, and fares hard, but is well satisfied with his lot, till, at last, finding his hunger grow importunate, he is told by " Work " that he may go for a while to " Repose," who will feed him better, and allow him a little pastime. " Soing " and " Cure," " Carefulness " and " Heed," let him out of the castle, not without some good advice, and a pluck of the ear from each. He tells his wife of all that had befallen him, speaking of it as if it were a dream. She would fain dissuade him from his good resolutions, but he determines not to listen to her, and concludes with a prayer that he may have firmness to persevere.

The style is of the homeliest throughout ; but there is the good meaning of the writer, worthy of the age of Louis the Just, and here and there an arch phrase, or a quaint old word, cunningly set, to repay the reader for his trouble.

Much the same may be said of his three other books which I have mentioned before.

The first, " Les Abus du Mõde Nouvel " is a strange farrago. Near the beginning, indeed (leaf the third, for the book is not paged), there is something better. It is the description of his musing himself to sleep at a little village, lulled by the song of a nightingale, and is quite in the taste of Chaucer. At waking he hears most dreadful cries, uttered by many " honourable persons," and " a gay spirit " named " Entendement," " Understanding," appears, and, furnishing him with pen, ink and paper, bids him commit to writing the vision he sees. A church then rises before him, built in strange guise ; through the door of which a cruel and dangerous man is thrusting himself by force. He holds a spit, "broche," with crosses, mitres, abbeys and bishoprics on it, which two women are endeavouring by force or sleight to drive into the church. "Entendement" launches forth into an invective against the abuses of the clergy. This is followed by a satire on the other vices of the time. At length Louis XII appears to him with Justice at his side, and he sees in a vision the conquest obtained by that monarch over the Venetians in 1509, and is proceeding to enlarge on the affairs of Italy, when Entendement says to him properly enough :

> Laisse ses guerres et puissantes victoires
> Aux croniqueurs pour mettre par histoire.

"Leave his wars and mighty conquests for chroniclers
        to record."

He then goes on to satirize the hypocrites (or bigots as he calls them) of both sexes ; and, from them, passes to the barbers, physicians, apothecaries, dancers, mummers, astrologers, gamesters, chemists, searchers after the philosopher's stone, forgers, priests, notaries, etc., etc. In the last leaf the book is presented to Jaques nomme de Touteville, counsellor and chamberlain to the King.

The next, the Contreditz du Prince des Sots, etc., consists of arguments for and against the different trades, professions and modes of life. These are introduced by Fantasy's conducting him to the forgery of Pallas, where he sees the apparatus that had been used for fabricating all the great writings in ancient times ; among the rest, the Speculum Vitæ of Roderic Zamora.

> And furthermore still there I found
> The fire all hot, where not long since
> Roderic of Zamora did found
> His human mirror : by heaven's prince,
> Matter so large and so profound
> I from that Spaniard's learning took
> That I thereon have wrought my book.

There were no less than five editions of the Speculum Vitæ Humanæ, besides a French translation of it, before the conclusion of the fifteenth century.

The arguments on merchandise, fol. 37, are in prose ; as is great part of the second book, de l'Estat civil. The tyranny of fashion over the Courtier's life is one of the most entertaining things in this work. (Fol. 171.)

Towards the end there is a brief eulogy on Saint Louis, and on the reigning monarch, Louis XII.

The last of the above-mentioned books, the Notables enseigneme˜s, etc., is, as the title imports, a collection of adages and proverbs : all of these are in quatrains. I should take this edition to be scarce : for De Bure has only the first (No. 3028 with an asterisk, in his Bibliographie), printed at Paris, without date ; but this has many additions. There is much wisdom in these, as there is in most sayings of this kind, but few readers I doubt are now willing to be at the trouble of " understanding a proverb, and the interpretation : the words of the wise and their dark sayings." A scantling of these therefore will suffice, and they shall be such as,

to make them the more palatable, contain some curious
intimation of the manners and customs of those times.

> Some chose the lowly villain's servile state,
> Their love of fields, and thorps and burghs so great ?
> Others prefer the court ; but blest are they
> Who safe in towns do pass their lives away.

> There are who fondly do their houses paint
> With signs armorial trick'd in colours quaint,
> And names and surnames mark'd in divers scrolls ;
> There are walls pictured by the hands of fools.

> Unwise the man who heareth Mass, I wist,
> With hound in leash, or hawk upon his fist ;
> He comes not into church to worship there,
> But to disturb his neighbours at their prayer.

> The lepers by the warning clack are known,
> As by his pig Saint Anthony is shown ;
> The inky cloak makes not the monk devout,
> Nor trappings proud the soldier brave and stout.

> He who at morn and eve would duly know
> How news and scandal with his neighbours go
> May of such idle chit-chat have his fill
> At barbers' shops, the oven, or the mill.

Pierre Gringore died about the year 1545.

THE END